And THE KING shall do according to his will; and he shall exalt himself, and magnify himself above every god, and shall speak marvelous things against the God of gods, and shall prosper *till* the indignation be accomplished: for that that is determined shall be done.

(Daniel 11:36)

THE ANTICHRIST KING — JUAN CARLOS?

As Heavily Documented By

DR. CHARLES R. TAYLOR

President, Today in Bible Prophecy, Inc.

Published by
BIBLE PROPHECY FOR TODAY
P.O. Box 5700, Huntington Beach, California 92615
ISBN 0-937682-15-2

FLAGS OF A UNITED EUROPE

E. C. Headquarters in Brussels, Belgium

Table of Contents

THE ANTICHRIST KING — JUAN CARLOS

Introduction

THE REASON for this very highly documented presentation is to give to you officially verifiable news reports that show to all people that King Juan Carlos I of Spain may be the endtime king, or emperor, of the prophesied Revived Roman Empire of the Tribulation Period: the king that commonly is referred to as "the antichrist."

MANY BIBLE REFERENCES are being fulfilled by THIS KING OF SPAIN. His father, Don Carlos, was rejected by Spain's exiled Queen Victoria Eugenia and by Pope Pius XII, both at the time of the birth and christening of Juan Carlos in 1938 and again in 1948 when Prince Juan Carlos was sent to Madrid to military genius Generalissimo Francisco Franco to begin his academic and military training to become the next king of Spain. (Juan Carlos' father, Don Carlos, was not born in Rome and was pro-communist.)

Read, or listen to, the extensive reasons and biblical correlations that verify that King Juan Carlos fits every Bible prophecy pertaining to "the king" of "the time of the end" as recorded in Isaiah, Ezekiel, Daniel, the Gospels and in The Revelation.

The time is at hand. This man stands before the world today as the strongest monarch of Western Europe, ready to be proclaimed king of the biblically prophesied Revived Roman Empire as soon as all of the true believers in Jesus Christ as Redeemer have been "caught up in the clouds to meet the Lord in the air" at the Rapture of the Church. He THEN will be given his "power and strength" by the leaders of the Western European nations that have ruled "with" him

(Rev. 17:13) and can then proceed to sign the JERUSALEM COVENANT (Dan. 9:27), guaranteeing Israel's security, and "the time of the end" will be in process.

May this treatise be a blessing to you and a means of helping you to reach many lost souls for Jesus (having within it verifiable proof of "the signs of the times") in these closing days of the Church Age. Then will come the seven years of the Tribulation Period, after which Jesus will come as King of kings and Lord of lords, will destroy all evil armies at the Battle of Armageddon and will establish His wonderful kingdom of "Peace on Earth."

SPREAD THIS WORD ABROAD, FOR EVERY WORD OF IT IS TRUE.

KING JUAN CARLOS I de BORBON y BORBON

Preface

There is to be an antichrist king who will have great authority during the last seven years of "the times of the Gentiles." In the years of his preparation, Dan. 9:26 refers to him as "the prince who shall come," and prophesies that he is to be of "the people" who destroyed the city (Jerusalem) and the sanctuary. This was done by Titus, a Roman general, in A.D. 70, establishing the fact that the prophesied end-time king is to be of the Roman empire. That is just one of many prophecies concerning "the king" who "shall exalt himself, and magnify himself above every god, and shall speak marvelous things against the God of gods, and shall prosper till the indignation be accomplished (at the end of the Tribulation Period -Dan. 11:36).

King Juan Carlos I of Spain was born in Rome, Italy, on January 5, 1938 and is a citizen of Rome as well as a citizen of Spain. That, however, is only one of the Bible declared factors of the end-time king's identity. He does much to confirm that he could be the one who may soon be called "the antichrist" as he fulfills many of the prophecies concerning the king that the Book of Revelation refers to as "the beast."

THE ANTICHRIST KING is to come on the world scene at God's appointed time and is to appear as a friend of Israel, signing a covenant to guarantee Israel's security for seven years (a week of years per Dan. 9:27). In the midst of that week - after 3½ years - he will become indwelt by Satan and will turn against the Jews, walking into their rebuilt temple in Jerusalem and declaring himself as God

(2 Thess. 2:4). All who refuse to worship him and receive his "mark of the beast" will be ordered to be slain.

How near are we to the beginning of that which the Bible refers to as "the time of Jacob's trouble" (Jer. 30:7 & Dan. 12:1) and commonly referred to as the Tribulation Period? The purpose of this treatise is to show that we are "standing at the doors" (Matt. 24:33) and that God's great prophecies are coming to pass today in great precision; and that many of those prophecies have to do with the end-time king and his exploits. King Juan Carlos I of Spain fits every category and appears to be that king. Listen to the many documentations of this book or hear them on the cassettes and realize that "the time is at hand" and the Tribulation Period about to begin.

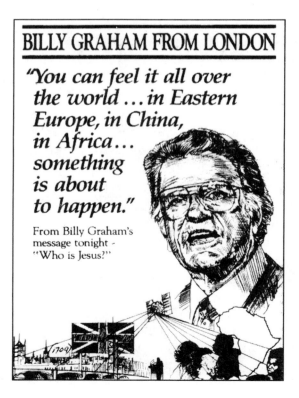

BILLY GRAHAM FROM LONDON

"You can feel it all over the world ... in Eastern Europe, in China, in Africa... something is about to happen."

From Billy Graham's message tonight - "Who is Jesus?"

Chapter One

THE MAN WITH THE POTENTIAL

In 1993, the signs are so overwhelming that King Juan Carlos I of Spain could be the man who is soon to be appointed, acclaimed or crowned king, or even Emperor of the Western European revised and revived Roman Empire and become, therefore, the Antichrist of the Tribulation Period that I must present for your enlightenment and assurance "the preponderance of the evidence" that this statement is verifiably true. I first wrote of him *in 1974* in my book entitled *Get All Excited - Jesus Is Coming Soon,* giving 16 pages of material under the heading:

THE MAN WITH THE POTENTIAL

No man in history has had so much potential, such training and such a position as does Prince Juan Carlos de Borbon, king-designate of Spain (in 1974).

The law of Spain requires that "a king must be of royal blood, at least 30 years of age, a Catholic and must swear allegiance to the National Movement which is Spain's only legal political organization."

Prince Juan Carlos of Borbon (the former royal Bourbon family of France) is the grandson of King Alfonso XIII and of Queen Victoria Eugenie of Battenberg (who was a member of the British royal family and a grand-daughter of Queen Victoria, the renowned Queen of England). King Alfonso XIII was exiled from Spain on April 14, 1931, when Spain was declared a republic.

Juan Carlos was born in Rome, the son of Prince Juan de Borbon of Battenberg and Princess Maria de las Mercedes de Borbon of Orleans on January 5, 1938. He spent his early years in Italy and in Switzerland, but in 1948 (the year in which Israel became a nation) his father met with Generalissimo Francisco Franco on the Portuguese border and agreed that Juan Carlos should be educated in Spain. Don Juan remained in self-imposed exile in Portugal.

In 1945, Don Juan, pretender to the throne of Spain, sent a manifesto to Franco in which he suggested that Franco resign. Two years later, when the Law of Succession to the Throne was adopted, article 13 of that law stated: "The head of state... may propose to the Cortes that there be excluded from succession those royal persons... who, because of their acts, deserve to lose the rights of succession established in this law."

In December, 1954, Don Juan acknowledged his rejection and agreed with Franco that Juan Carlos, then 16, should be the presumptive heir.

On Wednesday, *July 23, 1969*, Generalissimo Francisco Franco stood before a jam-packed session of the Spanish Cortes (Parliament). A detailed report printed in NEWSWEEK* stated that "in a barely audible voice" he "launched into a historic speech."

> "As always, the 76-year old Caudillo remained firmly in control of himself — that is, until he came to the reason for his rare public appearance. Suddenly his voice began to quaver, tears welled up behind his gold-rimmed spectacles and his hands shook violently. 'The relief of the Chief of State is a normal act imposed by man's mortality,' he declared. 'Conscious of my responsibility before God and history, I have decided to recommend Prince Don Juan Carlos de Borbon y Borbon as my successor.'

"Moving as it was, the announcement came as no surprise. For it had been an open secret for days that the 31-year-old Prince would be named by Franco to assume the vacant Spanish throne... Thus as Franco glared from a gilded seat on the podium, an open roll call was ordered—and Juan Carlos was overwhelmingly approved as Spain's next Chief of State.

"*Oath:* The next day, Franco returned to the Cortes, this time with the young Prince in tow. Dressed in the uniform of an army captain, Juan Carlos sat nervously until the moment came for him to receive the oath. 'Do you,' asked Cortes President Antonio I. Banales, 'in the name of God and the Holy Gospels swear loyalty to his excellency the Chief of State and the principles of the National Movement and the fundamental laws of Spain?' 'Yes, I do so swear,' the Prince replied. Then after a brief acceptance speech, he turned on his heels and followed Franco out of the hall..."

*Copyright. Newsweek, Inc.—1969.

THE TRAINING OF JUAN CARLOS

Juan Carlos was raised as a Roman Catholic. This was by the choice of his Catholic parents, but also was a prerequisite to the right to the throne of Spain.

It is of interest to discover, however, that the branch of Roman Catholicism in which he was raised and to which he ascribes is one which is listed only among "Roman Catholic Religious Orders of Men." Under this heading, it is named under the sub-heading of "Secular Institutes of Men" and as follows: "Opus Dei (Priestly Society of the Holy Cross) — 1928" (Date of its official recognition).

OPUS DEI

The Sacerdotal Society of the Holy Cross and Opus Dei (God's Work) originated in Madrid in 1926. Concerning the

Opus Dei, the following UPI dispatch from Madrid, printed in the Los Angeles Times, October 7, 1968, gives some very enlightening information:

"Madrid (UPI) — It is formally known as the Sacerdotal Society of the Holy Cross and Opus Dei. It is known popularly simply as Opus Dei. It is irreverently referred to as 'God's Octopus.'

"Opus Dei (God's Work) is an influence in the Spain of today. It is expected to be a leading voice in the Spain of tomorrow.

"At Opus Dei's large information center in Madrid, the organization is described as strictly a religious one and spokesmen vigorously deny charges by some Spaniards that it engages in outright political activity.

"Opus Dei was founded in this country in 1928 by a Spanish lawyer turned priest, the Rev. (now the Rt. Rev. Msgr.) Josemaria Escriva de Balaguer y Albas. It is a society of priests and laymen in which the guiding philosophy is that any human activity can be divine — that operating a computer or a lathe, or running a home, can be as sacred vocations as the priesthood. Members come from key sectors of commerce, industry, journalism, education and many other walks of life.

"Although now international *with headquarters in Rome,* directed by Msgr. Escriva, Opus Dei still has more power in Spain than in any other country. Members of the organization or sympathizers command:

"—Four cabinet portfolios, with control of the Spanish economy.

"—Three places in the 'shadow cabinet' of royal pretender Don Juan. (In addition, an Opus Dei priest is confessor to Juan Carlos, Don Juan's son, who is a possible future monarch).

"—Well-produced newspapers, radio stations, a news magazine and a leading news agency.

"—The nation's only non-state university, at Pamplona, considered one of the best in Spain; a business school associated with Harvard, an agricultural college and scores of schools and technical education centers.

"—Banks, insurance firms, real estate interests and a large industrial empire...

"For a variety of dogmatic and personal reasons, Opus Dei has aroused the hostility of both anticlericals and orthodox Roman Catholics, the latter seeing the society as a threat to Spain's arch-conservative religious tradition.

"The corporate structure and un-Spanish discipline of the society have begotten such unkind epithets as 'Holy Mafia' and 'White Freemonsonry'..."

From the above information, printed in 1968, it is noted that even at that time the Opus Dei organization was well entrenched in powerful places in business, education, news media and in high governmental positions, and even in the potential cabinet of the anticipated monarch. And in the event of the by-passing of Don Juan, which did occur, it is noted that the priest-confessor to Juan Carlos (the person most influential in the life of a devout Catholic) was an Opus Dei priest. The intent of such an organization can hardly be overlooked. This has a bit of verity in the following news item:

NEWSWEEK,* July 28, 1969 — "Pressure Group: The designation of Juan Carlos as future king was interpreted as a victory for Opus Dei, a Catholic lay order that constitutes Spain's most influential pressure group...

"As for the outlawed opposition parties, they are far too weak and fragmented to stand in Juan Carlos's way… 'The Prince is charming, unassuming and certainly not stupid,' said one foreigner who met Juan Carlos recently…"

*Copyright, Newsweek, Inc.—1969.

GENERALISSIMO FRANCISCO FRANCO

Prince Juan Carlos was under the personal supervision and instruction of military genius Generalissimo Francisco Franco from the moment Don Juan turned him over to Franco in 1948 when Juan Carlos was only 10 years old.

It was during the Spanish civil war (1936-1939) that Franco displayed his military prowess when he led his troops against great odds and defeated the Popular Front movement composed of Communists, Socialists, Republicans and anarchists. He drew men from Italy and Germany and defeated a coalition of men drawn from France, Russia and Mexico plus some American mercenaries. He fought in the air and on the ground. He was a flying general and a military strategist. When he captured Madrid and took complete control on March 28, 1939, he was named caudillo, or leader of the nation, Chief of State, Commander in Chief, Prime Minister and head of the Falange party. This is the man to whom Don Juan entrusted the training of his son, Juan Carlos.

MILITARY BACKGROUND

Gen. Francisco Franco undoubtedly had many long talks and discussions with Juan Carlos. But more than that, he saw that he received extensive academy training. Franco personally supervised .Juan Carlos' schooling and in due time saw his young protege graduate from the naval academy, the air force academy and rank third in a class of 271 at Saragosa Military Academy.

Carlos took extra graduate work at Madrid University and served apprenticeships in various government positions. He was considered "safe" by those who wished the authoritarian regime to continue in Spain.

When Juan Carlos took the oath of succession to the throne in the grand hall of the Cortes, the Spanish Parliament building, he was dressed in the uniform of an army captain. He knelt before a cross and swore his allegiance to his country, the National Movement and the Catholic faith.

Later, when the Prince of Spain signed the acceptance of succession in Zarzuela Palace, his state-owned residence in a suburb of Madrid, we wore the white uniform of a naval lieutenant. Carlos also holds the rank of captain in the air force.

Prince of Spain Juan Carlos de Borbon is extremely well qualified to serve as an officer and a military leader as well as a Chief of State a king.

THE SPEECHES OF PRINCE JUAN CARLOS

The manner of a man can often be determined by the over-all content of what he says. Carlos remains mostly in the background, for he knows that he must keep the favor of Gen. Francisco Franco and of the leaders of Spain if he is to be honored when the time comes for him to become King of Spain. His words are necessarily well chosen. The following excerpts are documented statements made by Prince Juan Carlos:

> "In this hour, I ask God's help, and I do not doubt he will give it, as I am sure we will be deserving of it by virtue of our conduct and work."
>
> June 12, 1970 (in interviews inside the palace):
>
> "I realize my position is a delicate one. I understand that I must be patient. It would serve no purpose to aggravate suspicions and animosities.
>
> "I know that some men do not agree with Franco that the monarchy should be restored. But I know I can

demonstrate that the monarchy can be a strong influence for order and progress."

Juan Carlos has said, "I will remain above the political scene if I am to have any real influence. I want to be a representative of the people — *all* the people."

Ray McHugh, chief of the Washington Bureau of Copley News Service, in a special article about the Prince, wrote: "Juan Carlos acknowledges that he is Franco's heir, but he says it is more important that he is the 'heir of Spain.'" He continues:

> "...the prince... has been known here as 'the boy' ever since Franco began to groom him for a king's role more than 20 years ago...
>
> "His life in Franco's shadow and his acquiescence to a carefully controlled environment have led some to decide that Juan Carlos is a man of small stature—a friendly, likeable young fellow, but one who lacks the fire and determination to play a major role in the continuing evolution of Spanish life.
>
> "Those who judge him in this fashion may be surprised. *Many visitors see steel beneath the boyish exterior. The fact that Juan Carlos has survived Franco's rigid training period, has graduated from all three of Spain's service academies and has reached the door to the throne room suggest determination and courage...*"

MORE OPUS DEI POWER

Don Cook, the Times' bureau chief in Paris, went to Spain. His dispatch from Madrid, printed in the Los Angeles Times, November 9, 1969, barely made more than three months after Prince Juan Carlos took his oath of succession, stated in part:

> "The shakeup Franco has carried out is particularly remarkable because it marks the virtual extinction of

the fascist Falange Party as the ruling force in Spanish politics...

"The rising force in Spain for the last decade has been the Opus Dei movement—a kind of vague Free Masonry of young, more modern-minded liberal Catholic technocrats. As political parties are banned in Spain except for the Falange, Opus Dei is not political nor is it a party, but it is, nevertheless, a considerable force in Spanish political life, as Franco's sweeping political changes attest.

"All the old Falangist ministers have been dropped...

"Franco, whose sense of political timing in Spanish affairs is as masterful as Gen. DeGaulle's was in France, kept the old cabinet going until the Falange ministers had bickered themselves into a situation where they had discredited themselves. Finally, Franco, at the urging of his vice president and close associate, Vice Admiral Carrero Blanco, who is prime minister in all but title, moved in with a clean sweep.

"Only four of the 18 cabinet posts were unaffected by the changes, and most important of all was the switch of the Opus Dei minister for industry, Gregorio Lopez Bravo, to the Foreign Ministry, and a move up the ladder for Laurento Lopez Rodo, another Opus Dei member who becomes secretary to the presidency—a kind of upper cabinet director. Lopez Rodo is generally given credit for having masterminded *the Opus Dei political strategy in the long power struggle which is now resolved...*

"The Opus Dei men are younger, more modern in their ideas and more efficient in their operation... They are also more pragmatic in foreign policy questions, and have already made it clear that *they intend to put relations with Europe and the Common Market in the fore-front of their policy...*"

OPUS DEI SPAIN'S FOREIGN OUTREACH

Within three months of the shakeup of the cabinet ministers of Spain, the new men in office were making strides toward NATO and the Common Market. In February, 1970, it was announced that Spanish Foreign Minister Gregorio Lopez Bravo had begun talks in Paris with French government officials on bringing his country into close cooperation with France and Western Europe.

On August 9, 1970, Bravo returned to Madrid from Washington and said the new U.S. bases pact will partially tie Spain to the North Atlantic Treaty Organization.

"It is contemplated in the new accord that we will be tied to NATO's new alert network by way of its aerial security system," he said.

Prince Juan Carlos visited Washington in the fall of 1970 at President Richard Nixon's invitation.

A few months later, the Washington Post carried an article to the effect that "President Nixon and his administration have been conducting a low key campaign to encourage Generalissimo Francisco Franco to step down and to name Prince Juan Carlos de Borbon y Borbon chief of state and king of Spain in the near future," according to informed sources.

> The same article dated August 5, 1971, stated:
>
> "The caudillo… surprised foreign embassy political analysts and Spanish politicians in early July when he suddenly issued a decree that will make the Prince acting chief of state if Franco becomes ill or travels abroad."
>
> Toward the close of that extensive report was the following statement:
>
> "Another reason the Administration wants an orderly transition is Spain's position at the extreme flank of the western Mediterranean. U. S. military

planners regard the country as a bastion in the face of
the Soviet naval presence in the Mediterranean, and as
a last-ditch line of defense against any possible land
war against the Soviet Union in Europe."

An earlier Associated Press dispatch from Washington had
stated that the Nixon administration plans to upgrade U. S.
military capability in Spain by dispatching 72 new F-4
Phantom fighters to the Air Force base at Torrejon. Involved
is the Air Force's 401st Tactical Fighter Wing at Torrejon
near Madrid.

One official is quoted as saying, pointing to a map of the
Mediterranean, that a simple glance at the southern flank of
NATO reveals that the United States must have the capability
of reinforcing there in any war.

The United States also has a naval base at Rota, Spain, you
will recall, for the servicing of our nuclear-equipped Polaris
and Poseidon submarines.

Other reports state that the United States has provided
$702 million in direct American aid to Spain since
1953—partly for air and naval bases in Spain. This aid is in
addition to various loans made to that country, and also the
loan of 10 destroyers and two submarines authorized on
April 9, 1972.

The former chief of naval operations, Vice Admiral
Carrero Blanco, became Gen. Francisco Franco's prime
minister and the head of Spain's only political party, the
National Movement, having taken over those positions in
special ceremonies on June 9, 1973. The naming of Carrero
Blanco to these posts was the expected first step toward
solving the problem of the succession in Spanish government.

It was Adm. Blanco who was instrumental in the official
naming of Juan Carlos de Borbon as the future king of Spain.

So strong had the "Opus Deistas" become by this time,
that one of the first changes made by the new premier was to
remove Foreign Minister Gregorio Lopez Bravo from office.

He replaced him, however, with an equally strong "Opus Deista" man, the former planning chief, Laureano Lopez Rodo. The next moves? Each step seems to make the Opus Dei conglomerate just another step closer to absolute control.

And Prince of Spain, Juan Carlos, has been under the direction of the Opus Dei priesthood continuously since his birth in Rome on January 5, 1938.

THE SIGNIFICANCE OF ROME

I've included this chapter on Prince Juan Carlos to show the very high potential for the soon fulfillment of climactic prophecies of the Bible.

The primary significance is not that Juan Carlos is fully trained to become the king of Spain, but that he does have sufficient military, air force, naval and strategic command training to be a potential leader for the entire Western European union of nations.

Bible prophecies state that such a ruler will come forth "in the latter years" and "at the time of the end."

Daniel 9:26 refers to "the prince who shall come," and we can most certainly see that Juan Carlos is not only a potential king, but that he has been, ever since 1948, a prince in preparation.

"The prince who shall come" is described in much more forceful terms in Daniel 11:36. In that verse he is called "the king."

> "and the king shall do according to his will; and he shall exalt himself and magnify himself above every god, and shall speak marvellous things against the God of gods…"

2 Thessalonians 2:3-9 refers to the coming monarch as "that man of sin" and as "the son of hell who exalts himself above all that is called God, or that is worshiped, so that he, as God, sits in the temple of God, showing himself that he is

God... Whom the Lord shall consume and shall destroy (ultimately) with the brightness of His coming. It shall be even him whose coming is after the working of Satan with all power and signs and lying wonders."

Earlier in this chapter, I said "it is conceivable that the end time leader does not yet know his full destiny. Revelation 13 says the dragon (the Devil, Lucifer, Satan) will give him 'his power, and his throne, and great authority.'" This is a valid statement. I have sought only to reveal the very strong evidence that Prince Juan Carlos, so far, may fulfill the prophetic picture.

Further verification also can be given.

Chapter 17 of the Book of Revelation gives us another look at this "prince who shall come." In this chapter, the Lord uses an allegory in which He portrays a scarlet colored beast coming forth, having seven heads and 10 horns, and having a woman riding upon his back. The Apostle John was astounded at what he saw, for we read in Revelation 17:7,

> "And the angel said unto me, Why did you wonder? I will tell you the meaning of the mystery of the woman, and of the beast that carried her, which has the seven heads and ten horns."

Verse 9 says that the mind that has wisdom will understand that "The seven heads are seven mountains on which the woman sits." Geographically, the city of Rome is actually built upon seven hills or mountains. Verse 18 verifies the fact of this interpretation: "And the woman whom you saw is that great city, which reigns over the kings of the earth."

At the time when John wrote the Book of Revelation, Rome was in full power as the sixth great empire of God's prophecies.

The beast has already been defined as being the ruling entity. The woman has now been defined as having identity with Rome. Next, let us consider the significance of this "woman" from Rome.

"THE WOMAN" FROM ROME

The description of this prophesied "woman" from Rome is not a pleasant one. Here is the prophecy as recorded in Revelation 17:4-6:

> "And the woman was clothed in purple and scarlet color, and was brazenly laden with gold and precious stones and pearls, having a golden cup in her hand, full of abominations and filthiness of her fornications;
>
> "And upon her forehead was a name written, MYSTERY, BABYLON THE GREAT, THE MOTHER OF HARLOTS AND ABOMINATIONS OF THE EARTH.
>
> "And I saw the woman drunk with the blood of the saints, and with the blood of the martyrs of Jesus; and when I saw her, I wondered with great amazement."

The sight was enough to amaze any Christian. Here were two astounding sights: a fierce-looking beast and a drunken and abominable woman coming forth together. The woman was seen to have costly garments and a golden cup; but the cup was filled with vileness and with the blood of the martyrs of Jesus. She was a fornicator—a partner of falseness.

This is *not* a picture of Roman Catholicism, as such. It is a portrayal of all false religions combined into one entity. It is a portrayal of the wretched endtime World Church System that will be set up "at the time of the end;" but it will have its seat of authority in Rome at the time of its revealing to the world as a whole, for this is specific Bible prophecy.

The church system will not honor Christ. It will, in fact, persecute those who worship Jesus Christ, for it is written:

"I saw the woman drunk with the blood of saints, and with the blood of the martyrs of Jesus."

That this does not represent orthodox Roman Catholicism is quite evident, for vast numbers of today's Catholics are true believers in the Lord Jesus Christ. But we must recall at this point that in accordance with many Scriptures, the identities of the beast and the woman are not to be revealed until after the true believers in Jesus Christ are "caught up together in the clouds to meet the Lord in the air" (1 Thess. 4:16-18 and 1 Cor. 15:51-57). The rapture of the Church will take place *before* the end-time king and his co-partner in crime, "the woman," are identified.

Only the Catholics who are not true Christians will be on hand. Those who really believe in Jesus as Saviour will have been "caught up" to be with the Lord.

JUAN CARLOS, OPUS DEI AND "THE WOMAN"

Bearing in mind that Juan Carlos was born in Rome and that the "Sacerdotal Society of the Holy Cross and Opus Dei" has its international headquarters in that city, let's investigate the matter further.

The fact that Juan Carlos is a member of Opus Dei already has been established. The term "member" is used because statistics show that new members join the Sacerdotal Society of Opus Dei by invitation only.

Let us note some of the precepts of the society.

Many articles have been published about the controversial Opus Dei. One of the more recent comprehensive articles was written by Times staff writer William Tuohy. It appeared in the June 24, 1973 issue of the Los Angeles Times:

"MADRID — The most controversial organization in Spain today is a powerful and sometimes mysterious Roman Catholic lay group called Opus Dei,

'God's Work." Critics call it 'Octopus Dei,' God's Octopus, or the 'Holy Mafia,' and charge that it exerts immense influence in Spanish economic, academic and political life.

"Further, the critics say, it is an elitist fraternity the members of which are selected not so much for religious vocation as for their wealth, brains, and even good looks…

"One conservative general described the movement as 'a new white Masonry that is trying to sow discord in the heart of the national institutions…'

"To Opus Dei followers, it simply pursues, in the words of its founder, Msgr. Josemaria Escriva y Balaguer, 'exclusively spiritual goals'… 'WE ARE NOT LINKED TO ANY COUNTRY, GOVERNMENT, POLITICAL MOVEMENT OR IDEOLOGY.'

"Says Opus Dei spokesman Miguel Alvarez, a well-dressed lawyer, in the order's Spanish headquarters just off fashionable Castellana Blvd., 'Our critics say that we are a secret organization, but here you are talking to me about Opus Dei. We have about 22,000 members in Spain and some 60,000 worldwide in 65 countries including the United States… People think we are powerful because some of our members are bankers and government officials… But critics never talk about the thousands of ordinary workers who are members.'

"Opus Dei was founded by Msgr. Escriva… in 1926, when the movement developed in the University of Madrid during the political ferment of that time…

"Msgr. Escriva… wrote what has become the Opus Dei bible: El Camino (the way) with 999 precepts — some simplistic, some complex, some ambiguous — for proper living. Samples:

"Maxim 78—'If you don't get up at a fixed hour you will not carry out your plan of life.'

"Maxim 720— 'O, my God, every day I am less sure of myself and more sure of thee.'

"Maxim 833 — 'Make your will virile in order that God will make you a caudillo (leader).'

"Maxim 941 — 'Obedience is the surest way. Obey your superior blindly. This is the way to holiness.'

"Originally printed in an edition of 2,000, El Camino has sold about 2,000,000 copies in several languages.

"In Opus Dei, there are various categories of membership... Some 'cooperators' can actually be non-Catholics. About two per cent to three per cent of the total membership are priests, Opus Dei officials say. New members join by invitation only: older members scout out likely prospects...

"In 1946, Msgr. Escriva moved to Rome where, according to Vatican sources, the top brass of the Catholic church was not altogether happy with the new organization. Nevertheless, Pope Pius XII recognized the order. But even today, sources say, the Vatican tends to frown on Opus Dei in Spain because officials believe, rightly or wrongly, that the organization is sometimes at odds with the more liberal prelates of the Spanish church, and it tends to support the regime for the sake of its own advancement..."

NOT TRULY "CHRISTIAN"

Although Opus Dei is recognized by a Christian church organization—Roman Catholicism—it is not, in the true sense of the meaning, a Christian movement.

Lip service is given, and it honors "the cross," but there is absolutely no evidence of any message of salvation through faith in Jesus Christ. On the contrary, it is very evident that this ultramodern movement bases its goals on "good works" alone.

A glance at the "maxims" which were quoted by Mr. Tuohy bears out this statement.

For further evidence, however, consider the following statements which are documented as the words of Prince of Spain Juan Carlos, an "Opus Deista."

> July 24, 1969, in his speech of acceptance as successor to the throne: "In this hour, I ask God's help, and I do not doubt He will give it, AS I AM SURE WE WILL BE DESERVING OF IT BY VIRTUE OF OUR CONDUCT AND WORK."

> June 12, 1970, in an interview in his palace in Madrid (note the emphasis on *his* endeavor): "I KNOW I can demonstrate that the monarchy can be a strong influence for order and progress… I MUST REMAIN ABOVE the political scene IF I AM TO HAVE ANY REAL INFLUENCE… I WANT TO BE A REPRESEN- TATIVE OF THE PEOPLE — ALL THE PEOPLE."

> July 24, 1969, in his acceptance speech before the Cortes: "I AM CLEARLY CONSCIOUS OF THE RESPONSIBILITIES I AM ASSUMING… I WANT TO SERVE MY NATION PUBLICLY, and for our people I WANT PROGRESS, DEVELOPMENT, UNITY, JUSTICE, LIBERTY *AND GRANDEUR…* "

THE REGAL JUAN CARLOS

Due to his present limbo position, the waiting monarch-to-be has made almost no public proclamations. He has wisely remained patiently subservient to Gen. Franco. He has, however, attended many state functions. He was a guest at the White House at President Richard Nixon's invitation.

Since he is a direct descendant of the famous Queen Victoria of England, he and his wife, Princess Sophia, (who is sister of the exiled King Constantine of Greece), were invited to Windsor Palace both for the silver wedding anniversary of Queen Elizabeth II and Prince Philip and for the huge party in honor of Lord Louis Mountbatten's 70th birthday.

The prince stands tall (6′3″) and stately. His training in all three of the branches of the armed services is reflected in his bearing.

There are many more things that could be said about this prince but the facts in this chapter are enough to inform and to warn you that there is a man who is right now well trained to become "the king" of the end-time 10-nation entity of Western Europe.

The prophets of God recorded it. Our Bible contains it. The Spirit is revealing it!

Since Bible prophecy specifically states that the one who is to be the end-time king cannot be given "his power, and his seat and great authority" until after "the rapture of the Church," it is indeed time to "GET ALL EXCITED — JESUS IS COMING SOON."

Third Cousin Queen Elizabeth II and Prince Philip
visit Spain's royal family in 1988

King Juan Carlos I addressing the Council of Europe

The King and Queen, accompanied by the President of Iceland, in the middle of the photograph, during the dinner she gave in their honour.

Chapter Two

WHAT ABOUT THE ASSYRIAN?

Many people ask about Assyria because of the prophecies in Isaiah pertaining to "the Assyrian" and his ultimate defeat at the coming of the Lord. This is a matter that requires study, but one that has definite and proper biblical answers, both historic and prophetic.

Seven hundred years before Jesus, Assyria was the primary enemy of the children of Israel, taking the ten northern tribes captive to Assyria in 721 B.C. and trying to capture Jerusalem in 710 B.C. In Isaiah 10, he wrote concerning Sennacherib, King of Assyria,

> O Assyrian, the rod of mine anger... I will send him against an hypocritical nation, and against the people of my wrath will I give him a charge, to take the spoil, and to take the prey, and to tread them down...
>
> Howbeit, he meaneth not so, neither doth his heart think so; but it is in his heart to destroy and cut off nations not a few. For he saith, Are not my princes altogether kings?...
>
> Shall I not, as I have done to Samaria and her idols, so do to Jerusalem and her idols?
>
> WHEREFORE it shall come to pass, that when the Lord hath performed his whole work upon Mount Zion and on Jerusalem, I will punish the fruit of the stout heart of the king of Assyria, and the glory of his high looks...

Shall the axe boast itself against him that heweth
therewith? Or shall the saw magnify itself against him
that shaketh it? As if the rod should shake itself against
them that lift it up, or as if the staff should lift up itself?

THEREFORE... the light of Israel shall burn and
devour his thorns and his briars in one clay.

This rebuke of the king of Assyria because of his boasting
against Jerusalem and the God of Israel and of Hezekiah,
King of Israel, came to pass. It is recorded in II Kings 19,
after "the great king, the king of Assyria" had said: "Who are
they among all the gods of the countries, that have delivered
their country out of mine hand, that the Lord should deliver
Jerusalem out of mine hand?"...the servants of king
Hezekiah came to Isaiah.

...And Isaiah said unto them, Thus shall ye say to
your master, Thus saith the Lord, Be not afraid of the
words which thou hast heard, with which the servants
of the king of Assyria have blasphemed me.

Behold, I will send a blast upon him, and he shall
hear a rumor, and shall return unto his own land; and I
will cause him to fall by the sword in his own land.[1]

And Hezekiah prayed before the Lord, and said, O
Lord God of Israel, which dwellest between the cheru-
bims, thou art the God, even thou alone, of all the kingdoms of the earth; thou hast made heaven and earth.

Now therefore, O Lord our God, I beseech thee,
save thou us out of his hand, that all the kingdoms of
the earth may know that thou art the Lord God, even
thou only.

(God's reply): Therefore thus saith the Lord
concerning the king of Assyria, He shall not come into

---

1. II Kings 19:5-7

this city. nor shoot an arrow there, nor come before it with shield, nor cast a bank against it. By the way that he came, by the same shall he return, and shall not come into this city, saith the Lord.

For I will defend this city, to save it, for mine own sake, and for my servant David's sake.

And it came to pass that night, that the angel of the Lord went out, and smote in the camp of the Assyrians an hundred fourscore and five thousand (185,000) soldiers; and when they arose early in the morning, behold, they were all dead corpses.

So Sennacherib king of Assyria departed, and went and returned, and dwelt at Nineveh. And it came to pass, as he was worshipping in the house of Nisroth his god, that Adrammelech and Sharezer his sons smote him with the sword: and they escaped into the land of Armenia, And Esarhaddon his son reigned in his stead.[2]

This is the end result of the first Assyrian, Sennacherib, who defied the Lord God, as recorded in the Bible. He lost his army of 185,000 men when God sent one angel against them in one night. The prophecy of Isaiah 10:27 came to pass,

And it shall come to pass in that day, that his burden shall be taken away from off thy shoulder. and his yoke shall be destroyed because of the anointing.

Similarly, in Isaiah 14, God refers to his protection of "my land," and of the defeat of the literal Assyrian, Sennacherib:

The Lord of hosts hath sworn. saying. Surely as I have thought, so shall it come to pass; and as I have purposed, so shall it stand:

2. II Kings 19:15, 19, 32-37

> That I will break the Assyrian in my land. and upon my mountains tread him under foot: then shall his yoke depart from off them, and his burden depart from off their shoulders.[3]

ISAIAH'S VIEW OF THE FUTURE "ASSYRIAN"

Just as the Assyrian of Isaiah's day lost his army and was defeated in one day, even so shall the ultimate enemy of Israel lose his army and be defeated in one day when the Lord returns to Jerusalem as Messiah, Deliverer and King of kings. God revealed this to Isaiah, and he recorded it in Isaiah 30:30-33,

> And the Lord shall cause his glorious voice to be heard, and shall shew the lighting down of his arm, with the indignation of his anger, and with the flame of a devouring fire, with scattering, and tempest, and hailstones.
>
> For through the voice of the Lord shall *the Assyrian* be beaten down, which smote with a rod...
>
> For Tophet (the lake of fire) is ordained of old; yea, for the king it is prepared; he hath made it deep and large: the pile thereof is fire and much wood; and the breath of the Lord, like a stream of brimstone, doth kindle it.

THE FULFILLMENT

The fulfillment of that prophecy is seen in Revelation 19:

> 11. And I saw heaven opened, and behold a white horse; and he that sat upon him was called Faithful

---

3. Isa. 14:24, 25

and True, and in righteousness he doth judge and make war. (At the end of Tribulation at second coming: not the rapture.)

15. And out of his mouth goeth a sharp sword,[4] that with it he should smite the nations: and he shall rule them with a rod of iron: and he treadeth the winepress of the fierceness and wrath of Almighty God.

16. And he hath on his vesture and on his thigh a name written, KING OF KINGS, AND LORD OF LORDS.

19. And I saw the beast, and the kings of the earth, and their armies, gathered together to make war against him that sat on the horse, and against his army.

20. And the beast (the endtime "Assyrian," the king of the tribulation era) was taken, and with him the false prophet that wrought miracles before him, with which he deceived them that had received the mark of the beast, and them that worshipped his image. These both were cast alive into a lake of fire burning with brimstone.

The place of the return of the Lord in power and glory as KING OF KINGS AND LORD OF LORDS is specified in the next to the last book of the Old Covenant, in Zechariah 14:

BEHOLD, THE DAY OF THE LORD COMETH, and thy spoil shall be divided in the midst of thee. For I will gather all nations against Jerusalem to battle...

Then shall the Lord go forth, and fight against those nations, as when he fought in the day of battle. And his feet shall stand in that day upon the mount of Olives, which is before Jerusalem on the east...and the Lord my God shall come, and all the saints with thee...

4. Defined in Heb. 4:12

> And the Lord shall be king over all the earth: in that
> day shall there be one Lord, and his name one...
> And it shall come to pass, that every one that is left
> of all the nations which came against Jerusalem shall
> even go up from year to year to worship the King, the
> Lord of hosts, and to keep the feast of tabernacles.

"The Assyrian" of ancient time was defeated when the angel of death slew 185,000 of his soldiers in one night, and when his own sons put him to death upon his return to his homeland of Assyria.

Similarly, "the Assyrian" enemy of the Lord's people, the antichrist king of the Tribulation Period will have his destruction when the Lord Jesus returns to earth in power and glory as KING OF KINGS preparatory to the establishing of His kingdom in Jerusalem when He shall reign in perfect peace and harmony for a period of one thousand years, commonly called "the millennium." What a day of rejoicing that will be!

WHO WILL BECOME "THE ASSYRIAN"?

In regard to the end time king who ultimately would desecrate the city of Jerusalem, Isaiah used the only term that he knew for the enemy of Israel, "the Assyrian;" for he lived many centuries before either the Greek or the Roman empires. For this reason, many people have had the mistaken idea that the antichrist king must come from the ancient Assyrian empire region of either Iraq or Syria.

DANIEL'S VISION OF RAM AND HE GOAT

Another reason for this error in theory is an improper interpretation of the vision that Daniel recorded in 538 B.C. In this God-given vision, Daniel saw a ram with two horns, and then he saw an he goat come from the west, having "a notable horn between his eyes." He watched as the goat came with rage against the ram and broke both of his horns, "and there was none that could deliver the ram out of his hand." [5]

In Dan. 8:16, the angel Gabriel was sent to him to "make this man to understand the vision." Starting with verse 19, he said:

> ...Behold, I will make thee know what shall be in the last end of the indignation: for at the time appointed the end shall be.
>
> The ram which thou sawest having two horns are the kings of Media and Persia.
>
> And the rough goat is the king of Grecia and the great horn that is between his eyes is the first king.
>
> Now that being broken, whereas four stood up for it, four kingdoms shall stand up out of this nation, but not in his power.
>
> And in the latter time of their kingdom, when the transgressors are come to the full, a king of fierce countenance, and understanding dark sentences, shall stand up.
>
> And his power shall be mighty, but not in his own power and he shall destroy wonderfully. and shall prosper, and practice, and shall destroy the mighty and the holy people.

THE FULFILLMENT OF THE VISION

This is a remarkable vision in that the king of Grecia, Alexander the Great, "the notable horn" of the vision, did not come into power and invade Media and Persia "from the west" for over 200 years. Daniel saw the vision in 538 B.C., and Alexander the Great did not conquer the Persian empire until 330 B.C.

---

5. Dan. 8:5, 7

That is as though Thomas Jefferson was predicting what President George Bush would do 200 years later!

Of even greater significance, however, is that the angel Gabriel explained to Daniel that after the notable one, Alexander the Great, had broken the power of the Medes and Persians, he would die without an heir and that his kingdom would be divided between his four generals. That came to pass in fulfillment of the vision, and Jerusalem was placed under Gen. Cyclops of the northern division, who controlled it until losing Palestine to Ptolomy I of Egypt in 301 B.C.

Egypt, as one of the great powers to rule over the city of Jerusalem during "the times of the Gentiles,"[6] controlled Jerusalem and most of Palestine from 301 B.C. until it was taken in conquest by the Seleucid division of the Greek empire led in 198 B.C. by Antiochus III.

At first, there was no persecution of the Jews under the Seleucid division of the Greek empire, but "in the latter time of their kingdom" there came on the historic scene Antiochus Epiphanes (175-164 B.C.). In 168 B.C., he attacked Jerusalem proper, destroyed all copies of the holy scriptures that he could find, burned a sow on the sacred altar to desecrate it and forbid the Jewish people to worship any gods but those of the Greeks. For a destructive period of 3½ years, he persecuted the Jews, being "of fierce countenance" and bent on destroying "the mighty and the holy people."[7] In fulfilling Bible prophecy by doing these things, he became *a primary type of the antichrist king* who is to come on the world scene during the Tribulation Period, for that man is to do the same things and to similarly desecrate the rebuilt Temple in Jerusalem, demanding blasphemous worship of himself as God.

The future phase of this prophecy is in verse 25 of Daniel 8.

6. Dan. 8:5, 7   7. Dan. 8:23, 24

> And through his policy (in the same manner as that of Antiochus Epiphanes) *also* he shall cause craft to prosper in his hand; and he shall magnify himself in his heart, and by peace shall destroy many; he shall also stand up against the Prince of princes; but he shall be broken without hand.

The prophecies here revealed to Daniel are all true, but they are multiple in nature and detail. First of all, he was told that the Greek empire would come on the scene and would obliterate that of the Persians. That was accomplished by 330 B.C.

The next is the most frequently misappropriated of the prophecies. It pertains to the desecration of the Temple and the subjugation of the Jewish people when they were forced to worship only the idols of the Grecians. Many of "the mighty and the holy people" were slain under the cruelty of Antiochus Epiphanes, who dominated Jerusalem particularly from 168-165 B.C. His tirades against God and his oppression of the Jews became so unbearable that Judas Maccabeus and his sons led a revolt that finally routed the Greek menace and gave the people of Israel a relative freedom. But another prophecy had been fulfilled, for it was, indeed, "in the latter time of *their* kingdom" (the kingdom of the four divisions of the Greek empire) that this occurred. Shortly thereafter the Roman legions came into the area and Jerusalem and the Jews came under their "protection."

THAT WHICH IS OVERLOOKED!

Since the future phase of the prophecy of Daniel 8 is in verse 25 and refers to the ultimate blasphemy when the antichrist king of the Tribulation Period will duplicate Antiochus' desecration of the Jewish Temple (that is shortly to be rebuilt in Jerusalem), doing so "through his policy:" that is, in the same manner as did the prototype, Antiochus Epiphanes, many people make the error of applying the entire passage to the end time king.

A careful analysis of the wording of the prophecy avoids this error, for it states quite clearly that the original desecration of the Temple is to occur "in the latter time of *their* kingdom," which definitely refers to the kingdom era of the four generals among whom Alexander the Great's empire was divided. It is *not* talking, at that point, about the end of the age (the Tribulation Period), but about the end of the era governed by the four recipients of the divisions of the Greek empire.

It was in "the latter time" of the Greek era when Antiochus Epiphanes dominated the region and desecrated the Jewish Temple in Jerusalem. That which the prophecy is proclaiming is that when the antichrist king comes on the scene (after the Church Age), he will conduct himself in like manner as did Antiochus: in other words, "through his policy."

Also relative to the antichrist, we read in II Thess. 2:4 that the wicked one "as God sitteth in the temple of God, shewing himself that he is God." It is also stated in Dan. 11:36,

> The king shall do according to his will; and he shall
> exalt himself and magnify himself above every god, and
> shall speak marvellous things against the God of gods,
> and shall prosper...

We see, therefore, that the end time antichrist king will seek glory and majesty and dominion as did Antiochus Epiphanes, but find no indication that he will come from the same area or location. He will not, in fact, come from any portion of the Greek empire (as some portray), for that would be contrary to the specific direction of the word of God.[8]

The prophecies concerning the region from which he will come all point to the Roman area, but not from the Greek portion thereof.

---

8. Dan. 7:8, 24

Chapter Three
GENTILE RULE OVER JERUSALEM

Gentile dominion over Jerusalem, the capital of Israel, began in 604 B.C. when King Nebudchadnezzar of Babylon conquered the city of Jerusalem and took most of the Jewish people, including the prophets Ezekiel and Daniel, into captivity.

In 603 B.C., this king had a God-given dream in which it was revealed that seven Gentile powers would rule over Jerusalem in a specific sequence. In Dan. 2:36-43, King Nebudchadnezzar's prophetic dream concerning these Gentile powers was portrayed as a multi-metallic image of a man. The head was of gold, the breast and arms of silver, the belly and thighs of brass, the legs of iron and the feet and toes were of iron mixed with clay. God gave the definition of this vision to Daniel, who described it as follows:

Item	Description	Fulfilled
Head of gold....	Nebudchadnezzar of Babylon Conquered Jerusalem, took Jews	604 B.C.
Breast & arms of silver	Darius the Mede conquered Babylon	539 B.C.
	Persia took over the Medes	529 B.C.
Belly & thighs of brass	Alexander of Greece conquered Persia	330 B.C.

```
                  Egyptian Ptolemy of Greek
                  Empire over Jerusalem ........................301 B.C.
                  Seleucid dynasty of Greek Empire .....198 B.C.
         Legs of iron .....Pompey of Rome entered Jerusalem....63 B.C.
                  Jews driven from Jerusalem
                  by Titus of Rome ..................................A.D. 70
                  Diaspora: Jews in Exile ..............A.D 70 - 1948
Feet & toes/
iron & clay........Revived Roman coalition
                  to rule Jerusalem .......................................Soon
```

Dan. 2:44 describes defeat of last Gentile power by Yeshua-Messiah at end of the "time of Jacob's trouble"[1] when Jesus comes as Messiah at end of Tribulation Period.

> And in the days of these kings shall the God of heaven set up a kingdom, which shall never be destroyed: and the kingdom shall not be left to other people (no more Gentiles), but it shall break in pieces and consume all these kingdoms, and it shall stand for ever.[2]

When Jesus returns to earth at His Second Coming at the end of the Tribulation Period, He will defeat the antichrist king at the Battle of Armageddon and will establish His righteous kingdom on earth, ruling from Jerusalem.

PROPHECY VERIFIED BY DANIEL'S VISION IN 541 B.C.

Daniel saw the same grouping of nations in his own vision 62 years later. In this vision, the empires were depicted as beasts rising out of the sea (of nations).

He recorded the vision in Dan. 7:3-27, summarized as follows:

1. Jer. 30:7   2. Dan. 2:44

Description	Fulfillment
3. And four great beasts came up from the sea	The major empires
4. The first was like a lion	Symbol of Babylon 604 B.C.
5. The next was like a bear, "and it raised itself up on one side, and it had three ribs in its mouth"	Medes and Persians 539 B.C. Three divisions: Babylon, Media Persia, to 330 B.C.
6. After this... Another like a leopard, which had on the back of it four wings of a fowl: and the beast had four heads: and dominion was given unto it.	Jerusalem to Greece 333 B.C. four heads: four divisions of Greek empire after death of Alexander in 323 B.C. Jerusalem under Ptolemy of Egypt division 301 B.C. Under Seleucid division of Greek empire 198 B.C.
(Jerusalem freed from Antichus by Maccabees)	Free 163 B.C. to 63 B.C. Pompey of Rome 63 B.C.
7. Fourth beast with iron teeth... and it had ten horns.	Ten-nation revived Rome to rule Jerusalem... Soon

This correlates with John's vision of the scarlet colored beast of Revelation 17 wherein it is stated:

10. And there are seven kings: five are fallen, and one is, and the other is not yet come; and when he cometh, he must continue a short space (the final seven year era).	*7 kings:* 7 empires *5 fallen:* Babylon, Media, Persia, Greece, Egypt. *1 is:* Rome in John's day. *1 to come:* Revived Rome.

All prophecy correlates and comes to pass when studied with proper biblical understanding. Bible prophecy is inspired by the Lord God.

LAST RULER TO BE OF ROMAN AREA

In his description of "the prince who shall come" who becomes "the king" of the "short space" revived Roman empire, the length of time is defined in Dan. 9:27,

> And he shall confirm the covenant (of guarantee of security) with many (returned Israelis) for one week (of years - 7 years)...

Continuing with the description of Daniel's vision of the four beasts (major empires), the last one having ten horns:

> I considered the horns, and, behold, there came up among them another little horn, before whom there were three of the first horns plucked up by the roots: and, behold, in this horn were the eyes of a man, and a mouth speaking great things.[3]

Verse 24 picks up the definition:

> And the ten horns out of this kingdom are ten kings (rulers) that shall arise: and another shall rise after them; and he shall be diverse from the first and he shall subdue three kings.

How remarkable: the developments in the Western European Community today fit exactly with the prophecies given by the Lord God to Daniel more than 2,500 years ago! These prophecies are coming to pass in our generation! The king of the end time is about to come into power. His base of operation already is established.

LATEST PROGRESS TOWARD EUROPEAN UNION

May 19, 1993, Cox News Service: LONDON — In a sharp reversal of their decision a year ago, Danish voters Tuesday gave a final push to the movement for greater European unity. The nearly final tally showed a 56.8 percent to 43.2 percent vote in favor of the Maastricht Treaty on European unification.

---

3. Dan. 7:8

May 21, 1993, Los Angeles Times: LONDON — After months of debate, the House of Commons voted Thursday night to ratify the Maastricht Treaty on European unity. The bill now goes to the House of Lords, where its approval is expected.

Conservative Party leaders viewed the victory on behalf of European unity in the House - two days after it was approved in a referendum in Denmark - as completing approval of the Maastricht Treaty by the 12 members of the European Community.

COMMENT

The 12-nation E.C. now only needs Austria for #13 for Antichrist to reduce it to the final 10 — AFTER THE RAPTURE. JESUS IS COMING SOON!

REESTABLISHED ROME

In 57 B.C., Luxembourg and The Netherlands were overrun and became a part of the Roman Empire. Two thousand and five years later, on June 8, 1948 (the same year that Israel became a nation again after more than 2,500 years of exile), the Benelux Agreement was signed by Belgium, Luxembourg and The Netherlands as the "little three" nations began to patch things up after the devastations of World War II.

On March 25, 1957, these three nations brought in Italy, France and West Germany and signed the Treaty of Rome in Rome, Italy. This established the European Economic Community usually referred to as the Common Market. Reestablished Rome was on its way.

March 9, 1964, *Newsweek:* Progress was made in Brussels where the Common Market Council of Ministers voted to merge Western Europe's three most important supra-national institutions: the Coal-Steel

Community, the Atomic Energy Community (Eurotom), and the Market... The Brussels agreement fits well with the plans of General Charles DeGaulle... What the General is seeking is greater political cooperation among sovereign states.

June 15, 1964, *Newsweek:* Franco believes that DeGaulles vision of a confederated Europe... will emerge triumphant over Washington's fading dream of a vast Atlantic community. DeGaulle, in turn, sees Spain as an essential part of his confederated Europe...

March 15, 1965, *Newsweek:* ...the Common Market members... began negotiations aimed at bringing neutral Austria within the Market's structure.

January 1,1973, *World Almanac:* Great Britain, Denmark and Ireland formally entered into the European Common Market.

May 29,1979, *Los Angeles Herald Examiner:* Athens, Greece — Greece became the 10th member of the European Common Market yesterday culminating 22 years of effort by Premier Constantine Caramanlis to join his country economically with Europe. Greece's active membership is scheduled to start Jan. 1, 1981.

January 1, 1986, *Reader's Digest World Almanac:* Spain and Portugal join European Community: Become 11th and 12th members of European Economic Community Common Market.

TWELVE OUT OF THIRTEEN

A careful study of the Scriptures has revealed that "the king" of the Tribulation Period, the seven-year era to follow the rapture of the church, is to be a king who is to come into prominence after there are 10 members (the ten horns) in the revived Roman entity. Note again the specific statement of Dan. 7:24,

> And the ten horns out of this kingdom are ten kings
> that shall arise: and another shall rise after them; and
> he shall he diverse from the first, and he shall subdue
> three kings.

This king is to be "diverse from the first," and, therefore, is not to be one of the first ten members of the Treaty of Rome's Common Market. It would be contrary to the inspired Word of God, therefore, for this king to come from any portion of the Greek empire as some have implied, for Greece was the 10th member to join the Market.

Of further interest, there are to be 13 members in total, for after this king has come into his place of authority, he is destined to "uproot" (eliminate) three of the original members as specified in Dan. 7:8

> I considered the horns, and, behold, there came up
> among them another little horn, before whom were
> three OF THE FIRST HORNS plucked up by the
> roots...

THE REVISED TEN

Although three of the first ten are to be removed when the proper time comes, there is to remain a final 10-member coalition, for it is written in Rev. 17:14 that

> These (the 10) shall make war with the Lamb, and
> the Lamb shall overcome them: for He is Lord of lords,
> and King of kings...

The Lamb of God who is the Lord of lords, of course, is the returning Jesus, the Messiah, when He returns to the earth at His Second Coming. That coming of Christ is entirely different from His coming for His saints at the rapture of the church when they (we) are to be "caught up... in the clouds to meet the Lord in the air: and so shall we ever be with the Lord." That occurs just prior to the tribulation events.

WHICH NATIONS?

In the light of the specific prophecy that "he shall uproot three kings,"[3] it is an amazing factor that exactly three nations of the Common Market have given trouble almost from the beginning.

EXAMPLES:

April 1, 1985, *Arab News:* Ireland, the only member outside NATO, rejects possible cooperation in defense and security within the community, as do Denmark and Greece.

September 7, 1985, *The Economist:* A new Dutch text attempts to straddle remaining differences with an ingenious let-out clause on security issues that could satisfy neutral Ireland, legalistic Denmark and half-hearted Greece.

January 3, 1987, *The Economist:* Last-minute hitches in Ireland and Greece delayed ratification of the reform of the Rome treaty.

July 9, 1988, *Jerusalem Post:* The intifada is responsible for some diplomatic setbacks. It was either the direct cause, contributory factor or convenient excuse for the following:

The failure of Greece to keep its promise to raise its diplomatic relations with Israel to embassy level…

Ireland's continuing refusal to accept Israeli ambassador in Dublin.

When President Chaim Herzog visited Denmark last November, pro-Israeli feelings in that traditionally sympathetic country were at an all-time high. Now they are at an all-time low, with… anti-Israeli demon-

3. Dan.7:8

strations and wall graffiti becoming an almost daily
feature of Copenhagen street life...

We see, therefore, that three nations are contrary to NATO
and to defense and security measures by the Common Market
and that the same three nations also are contrary to Israel.

Inasmuch as the soon-to-be selected king of the European
Community (Common Market) is destined to covenant to
assure Israel's security, it is therefore evident that these are
the ones most apt to be opposed to such action, and, therefore, subject to be "uprooted."

In order for this to take place (three being eliminated and
yet leaving ten), there has to be a total of thirteen nations in
the Common Market. Today there are twelve.

WHO WILL BE NO. 13?

Three nations that were considered for membership in
1987 were delayed or refused.

April 15,1987, *Orange Co. Register:* ATHENS - In a move
that troubled Western Europeans and stirred debate on how
the continent is defined, Turkey applied Tuesday for full
membership in the European Economic Community.

Community officials said recently that the application
posed a problem for some Western Europeans who dispute
Turkey's basic eligibility, as a nation, with a Moslem majority
and with most of its territory in Asia.

May 2, 1987. *The Economist:* Turkey applied to become the
13th member of the Community despite near-universal hesi-
tation among the present members.

Few people expect Turkey to join the club this century.

October, 1987, *Europe Mag:* Norway is the next likely
candidate for membership of the European Community,
although politically this scenario is unlikely to ripen before
the early 1990s. No timetable for Norwegian membership is
openly discussed.

Dec. 16,1987, *Miami Herald:* In Brussels, the European Community refused to admit Morocco as a member of the trading bloc, but officials said the 12 members are willing to strengthen economic and political ties with the North African nation.

ALL SIGNS POINT TO AUSTRIA

Dec. 8,1986, *Financial Times:* Austria has been through a bad patch; but come the new year and the formation of a new government, the country could be off in fresh and more self-confident directions.

The big chances are likely to be a recognition that Austria is preeminently a Western European state or its future is bleak. The problem facing Austria is how to enter the mainstream of West European affairs, for that is where the majority of its leaders now see that it belongs.

Mar. 7,1988, *Insight:* As the European Economic Community has strengthened its ranks...This trend is leading Austrian politicians and citizens to realize they have little choice but to apply for full membership in the Common Market. Many Common Market members have been encouraging Austria to come aboard .

April 20, 1988, *Wall Street Journal:* Austria plans to decide whether to become a member of the Common Market in 1989.

April 1,1989, *The Economist:* An EFTA country, Austria, said it would apply for EEC membership.

Austria was a part of the old Roman empire, as also were Spain and Portugal, which were the last two to join the Common Market.

With these three in, and with Denmark, Ireland and Greece out, you have the perfect alignment for an exact fulfillment of the specific prophecies of Daniel in the Old Testament and of John in the Book of Revelation: a revived and revised ten-nation Roman empire.

Bible prophecy is coming to pass in great detail, and the "time of the end" is just around the corner. BELIEVE THE BIBLE! The Tribulation era king has no authority to make those changes until after we, the believing Christians, are taken "out of the way"[4] by way of the Rapture - SOON!

4. II Thess. 2:7

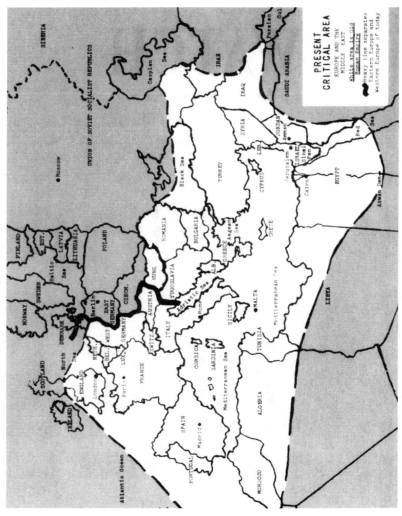

Area as of 1989

Chapter Four

THE OVERCOMER

Jesus said, "…In the world, ye shall have tribulation: but be of good cheer; I have overcome the world."[1]

…For whatsoever is born of God overcometh the world: and this is the victory that overcometh the world, even our faith.[2]

For by grace are ye saved through faith; and that not of yourselves: it is the gift of God: not of works, lest any man should boast.[3]

But thanks be to God, which giveth us the victory through our Lord Jesus Christ.[4]

Therefore being justified by faith, we have peace with God through our Lord Jesus Christ.[5]

…That if thou shalt confess with thy mouth the Lord Jesus, and shalt believe in thine heart that God hath raised him from the dead, thou shalt be saved.

For with the heart man believeth unto righteousness; and with the mouth confession is made unto salvation.[6]

For whosoever shall call upon the name of the Lord shall be saved.[7]

1. John 16:33
2. I John 5:4
3. Eph. 2:8, 9
4. I Corin. 15:57
5. Rom. 5:1
6. Rom 10:9, 10
7. Rom. 10:13

These are but a few of the tremendous promises of God.
Jesus promises the forgiveness of our sins and, as stated in
the introduction to this book, He promises to all those who
believe in, and place their trust in His atonement, a place
with Him in His Heavenly Home.

"We shall see the King some day" is not just a song: it is a
reality: and that Day is almost here.

WILL YOU BE READY?

When Jesus does come to resurrect all saints and to
redeem all living Christians, giving them (us) new, eternal
and perfect bodies that will be resurrection bodies that shall
live for ever, and He transports us up to God in the Rapture
of the church, will YOU be ready for that judgment day?

There is one requirement: your sins must be forgiven.

PSALM 103

Bless the Lord, O my soul: and all that is within me,
bless his holy name.

Bless the Lord, O my soul, and forget not all his
benefits:

Who forgiveth all thine iniquities (all your sins);
who healeth all thy diseases; Who redeemeth thy life
from destruction; who crowneth thee with loving kind-
ness and tender mercies;

Who satisfieth thy mouth with good things; so thy
youth is renewed like the eagle's.

He hath not dealt with us after our sins; nor
rewarded us according to our iniquities.

For as the heaven is high above the earth, so great is
his mercy toward them that fear him.

As far as the east is from the west, so far hath he
removed our transgressions from us.

Like as a father pitieth his children, so the Lord
pitieth them that fear him.

For he knoweth our frame; he remembereth that we are (made from) dust.

The Lord hath prepared his throne in the heavens; and his kingdom ruleth over all.

Bless ye the Lord, all ye his hosts; ye ministers of his, that do his pleasure.

Bless the Lord, all his works in all places of his dominion: Bless the Lord, O my soul.[8]

JESUS SAID

Let not your heart be troubled: ye believe in God, believe also in me.

In my Father's house are many mansions: if it were not so, I would have told you. I go to prepare a place for you.

And if I go and prepare a place for you, I will come again, and receive you unto myself; that where I am, there ye may be also...

I am the way, the truth, and the life: no man cometh unto the Father, but by me.[9]

I am the door: by me if any man enter in, he shall be saved, and shall go in and out, and find pasture...

...I am come that they might have life, and that they might have it more abundantly.

I am the good shepherd: the good shepherd giveth his life for the sheep...

I am the good shepherd, and know my sheep, and am known of mine...and I lay down my life for the sheep.

And other sheep I have, which are not of this fold: them also I must bring, and they shall hear my voice; and there shall be one fold, and one shepherd....

8. Psalm 103:1-5, 10-14; 19, 21, 22   9. John 14:1-6

And I give unto them eternal life; and they shall never perish, neither shall any man pluck them out of my hand.[10]

JESUS LOVES YOU

Jesus died for you and for me. His perfect blood that was shed on the tree (cross) of Calvary was given for our salvation.

Jesus lived the perfect life that you and I cannot live, and then gave His life as a ransom for our souls, that "Whosoever shall call upon the name of the Lord shall be saved." He paid the price. Jesus bought our ticket to His Heavenly Home when He gave His life for us; and God raised Jesus from the dead. We also receive eternal life *when* we ask the Lord to forgive our sins, because Jesus suffered and died in our place: *when* we accept that pardon provided by His sacrifice.

Will you receive Jesus as your Savior today? Do you want a full and complete pardon for all your sin so that you can be ready to go to God's perfect dwelling place in heaven?

God loves you and Jesus loves you. All that I can do is to introduce you to the Savior. His name is Jesus. He loves you so much that He took the punishment for all of your sins. Will you thank Jesus today? Make it official by saying, *in faith,* this prayer:

> Dear God and Father in Heaven: I thank you for sending your Son, Jesus, into this world to save for eternity all who would put their trust in Him. I have done wrong and I cannot save myself.
>
> Right now, I accept the fact that Jesus paid the price for my salvation when He died for my sins and for me. Forgive me, Lord. Let your Holy Spirit come into my heart this day, cleansing my life and setting me free

10. John 10:9-28

from the guilt and from the eternal punishment that I deserve. I am sorry for my sin. I ask Jesus right now for my salvation; and I thank Him for it. Thank you, Lord Jesus, for saving my soul. I will now love You as You guide my life by Your Holy Spirit. Amen.

That which you need to do now is to find a good church that believes all of the Bible, be baptized according to the command of the Lord as a witness to the world that you have been "buried with Christ in baptism and risen to new life in Him." Read your Bible every day, for it is your spiritual food and will be a constant blessing to you; and go on your way rejoicing in the grace and mercy of God, praising the Lord for His love and His salvation. Tell others about Jesus as you "Study (the Bible) to shew thyself approved unto God, a workman that needeth not to be ashamed, rightly dividing the word of truth."[11]

It is the Bible that contains all the promises of the coming of the Lord to receive all believing Christians unto Himself, that we might dwell for ever with Him in His Heavenly Home, and the fulfillment of the many prophecies of the Bible indicate that the coming of the Lord for us now is very, very near, Praise the Lord!

Trust in Him today!

THE DAY AND THE HOUR?

It has been stated so often that "No man knoweth the day or the hour when the Son of man cometh" that many people have the mistaken idea that we are not to know anything about the coming of the Lord or the revealing of Satan's substitute Antichrist. Much detail in the Bible, however, shows this to be a false conception. Jesus, Himself, said in

11. II Timothy 2:15

Mark 13:37, "And what I say unto you, I say unto all, Watch!" We are told to observe the "signs of the times" and to be His witnesses to all the world.

About one-third of the Bible is prophecy. Yes, we are to know that which is coming to pass, and to proclaim it. In I Thess. 5:4 it is stated,

> But ye brethren, are not in darkness, that that day should overtake you as a thief.

Beloved, we are to see and to know and to understand that God has given to us His Bible as our guide pertaining to His great Plan for all mankind. Notice how much information God has for us in II Thess. 2:1-8.

> Now we beseech you, brethren, by the (second) coming of our Lord Jesus Christ, and by our (final) gathering together unto him (when the last soul of the Tribulation has been won and the last martyr has been slain, and the bride of Christ "hath made herself ready," according to Rev. 19:7).
>
> That ye be not soon shaken in mind, or be troubled, neither by spirit nor by word, nor by letter from us, as that the day of Christ (Gr. Christos: the Messiah) is at hand.
>
> Let no man deceive you by any means: for that day (of Christ the Messiah's return as King of kings) shall not come, except there be a falling away (Gr. apostasia: defection from the truth as of the modernism and occultism of today) first, and that man of sin be revealed, the son of perdition (The one who shall become indwelt by Lucifer);
>
> Who opposeth and exalteth himself (becomes adverse to his first intent as a friend of the Jews, after being slain and indwelt by Lucifer-Satan at the middle of the Tribulation Period, as defined in Rev. 13:3 and 4,

And I saw one of his heads (the endtime king) as it were wounded to death: and his deadly wound was healed: and all the world wondered after the beast.

And they worshipped the dragon (Satan in him) which gave power (Gr. exousia: superhuman power and authority) unto the beast (the Tribulation king): and they worshipped the beast (with Lucifer-Satan now dwelling in him), saying, Who is like unto the beast? who is able to make war with him? (He comes back to life!)

...above all that is called God, or that is worshipped; so that he as God (which Lucifer has always wanted to be) sitteth in the temple of God, showing himself that he is God...

And now ye know what (who it is that) withholdeth that he might be revealed in his time.

For the mystery of iniquity doth already work (the spirit of antichrist already is in the world): only he who now letteth (hinders) will (hinder), until he be taken out of the way (When Jesus comes and calls "up" His Body, the Church, into heaven at the Rapture).

And THEN shall that Wicked (end-time king) be revealed (in all of his qualified authority for he has been in preparation ever since Israel was reestablished in 1948; having begun his training in the same year), whom the Lord shall (ultimately) consume with the spirit of his mouth, and shall destroy with the brightness of his coming (at the end of the Tribulation Period as revealed in Rev. 19 :11- 21).

THE MAN

That "man of sin" who is destined to be the beast-king and tool (subservient agent) of Lucifer-Satan for the entire Seven-Year Tribulation Period, being overcome and slain by Lucifer-

Satan at the middle of the era and physically indwelt and taken over by him for the last forty-two months thereof (Rev. 13:5), comes on the world scene as a man of high integrity, popularity and dignity, proclaiming peace and democracy as "his policy" (as of Dan. 8:25) and as his answer to the morass of world problems, yet capable of tremendous military strategy, power and authority. He does not suddenly appear on the world scene, but is a reigning and very popular king to whom the leaders of the Revived Roman Empire area of Western Europe will be anxious to turn to due to the sudden disappearance of millions of Christians - "at the time of the end" - when the Rapture has taken us Home to Glory.

The man just described in biblical terminology is possibly evident today as to his identity as the very popular and authoritarian King of Spain. He is the only man in the world who fulfills all of the prophesied factors and requirements listed relative to "the king."

WATCH, therefore, THE COMING KING!

It was almost prophetic that in the same year that the Treaty of Rome was signed in Rome, Italy, establishing the Common Market (1957), Henri Speak who then was Secretary General of NATO said in a speech:

> "What we want is a man of sufficient stature to hold the allegiance of all people and to lift us out of the economic morass into which we are sinking.
>
> "Send us such a man and be he god or devil, we will receive him."

Already, Prince Juan Carlos was in training to become the king of Spain. Now he is King of Spain and also "King of Jerusalem."

COINCIDENCE?

Does God work by pattern? In checking my previous news bulletins for the announcement of the selection of Prince

Juan Carlos to become the king of Spain, which was in 1969,1 found in Vol. 4, No. I Today In Bible Prophecy the following:

> Feb. 5, 1969, *Los Angeles Times:* CAIRO - The leader of the most militant Arab commando group has been elected chairman of the Palestine Liberation Organization. He promptly announced plans to escalate the armed struggle in all parts of "occupied Palestine."
>
> Mohammed Yasser Arafat, the leader and official spokesman of Al Fatah, the National Movement for the Liberation of Palestine, was chosen chairman of the PLO during a meeting here...What the Cairo meeting means, in effect, is that Al Fatah has taken control of the PLO.
>
> Feb. 17, 1969, *NEWSWEEK:*... Within hours of his election, Arafat... arrived at Cairo's Presidential Palace for a two-hour interview with Nasser. And when he emerged, Arafat took with him A PLEDGE FROM NASSER THAT ALL 7,000 PALESTINIAN TROOPS ATTACHED TO THE EGYPTIAN ARMY WOULD BE RELEASED TO FIGHT WITH THE COMMANDOS...
>
> Arafat himself declared last week, "Let the big powers decide what they like. We have already made our decision - A DECISION BASED ON THE GUN."

Thus it was that in the same year that Prince Juan Carlos was officially designated to become the next king of Spain, his counterpart was designated to be the leader of the PLO, an organization dedicated to the destruction of Israel, which Carlos is destined to defend.

COULD IT BE?

You have the Bible declarations that the king who ultimately shall be called the Antichrist ("beast" of Rev. 13 and

17) is to be of the Revived Roman Empire[12] and is to come into authority "after" ten nations have formed that entity.[13] The tenth nation, Greece, joined the Treaty of Rome's European Economic Community, the Common Market, on Jan. 1, 1981.

The next nations to join the E.C. after the formation of "the ten" were Spain and Portugal, which became members Jan. 1, 1986. One more, evidently Austria, is to join the E.C., making a total of 13; for it is written in Dan. 7:24 that "he" (the end time king of destiny) will "subdue three kings."[13] Dan.7:8 specifies that by him "three of the first" are to be "plucked up by the roots" - eliminated. News reports documented in Chapter 3 of this book identify these three as being, most assuredly, Denmark, Ireland and Greece. And, according to the Scriptures, it is to be the king of the 11th nation to join the Roman entity, the king of Spain, who will bring about the fulfillment of that prophecy. [14]

Consider now the amazing background, history, declarations of and accomplishments of the very popular King of Spain, King Juan Carlos I.

His entrance into the forefront of the world scene was as he desired: in grandeur. Here is a graphic report as of that date:

SPAIN, CATHOLIC CHURCH HONOR JUAN CARLOS

Nov. 27, 1975, *Los Angeles Herald & Examiner:*
MADRID, Spain (AP) - Flanked by European royalty and three Common Market presidents, King Juan Carlos received the highest blessing of the Roman Catholic Church and the cheers of thousands of countrymen today as Spain paid official homage to its new leader.

12. Dan. 9:26   13. Dan. 7:24   14. Dan. 7:8

Shouts of "Long Live Spain" and "Long Live the King" greeted the 37-year-old monarch and his wife, Queen Sofia, as they rode through the capital's streets to Mass at the 16th century Church of Los Jeronimos ahead of a full military parade.

The ceremony, one week after the death of the nation's longtime autocratic leader, Gen. Francisco Franco, underscored Europe's new view of Spain and the king's hopes to begin stepping toward democracy. The royal couple smiled and waved at the crowd from a closed car.

Inside the church, the biggest gathering (from 68 countries) of foreign dignitaries in Spain's history watched as the church's political voice, Vincente Cardinal Enrique y Tarancon, the liberal archbishop of Madrid, celebrated Mass of the Holy Spirit.....

Seated on the front rows were President Valery Giscard d'Estaing of France, West German President Walter Scheel and Irish President Cearbhail Odalaigh. Scheel was flanked by the Duke of Edinburgh, Britain's representative, and Prince Rainier of Monaco. U.S. Vice President Nelson Rockefeller was one row back.

ALSO KING OF JERUSALEM!

Since the Middle Ages, the kings of Spain have carried the additional title of "King of Jerusalem." This was verified by an official publication of the Roman Catholic Church on the day of the presentation of King Juan Carlos I at the ceremony in Madrid, recorded as follows:

> November 27.1975, *THE TABLET:* The swearing in of Prince Juan Carlos de Borbon as King of Spain automatically involved revival of an ancient title applied to Spanish monarchs, "KING OF JERUSALEM," according to the Spanish consul general there. Count de Campo

Rey said that the title, hereditary in Spanish royalty since the Middle Ages, "while merely honorific," today, was nevertheless "extremely precious." He said that "Catholic Kings" of Spain had been recognized by Popes and by Muslim rulers for centuries as "protectors of Catholic Holy Land interests," and that, although Spanish influence was later superseded partially by French, "certain sites and monasteries in the Holy Land" were still under Spanish protection.

King Carlos escorts frequent visitor in Madrid 6/16/93

King Carlos at ease with Italian president Nov. 1991

Chapter Five

THE KING AND THE COVENANT

SATAN IS A LIAR! In Rev. 12:9, he is referred to as "the great dragon, that old serpent, called the Devil and Satan, WHICH DECEIVETH THE WHOLE WORLD."

One of his greatest deceptions concerning the end times is the very false concept that when the "man of sin" is revealed to the world in general, he will make a covenant of peace with Israel, or else will bring about so great a covenant of peace between the Jews and the Arabs that he will be accepted by the Jewish people as their Messiah (Mosiach ben Joseph) and thusly become the producer of peace on Earth for the first 3½ years of the Tribulation Period.

Nothing could be further from the truth according to the order of events outlined in chapters 6 through 9 of the Book of Revelation, also being contrary to chapters 38 and 39 of Ezekiel and to many other Old Testament passages in Isaiah, Jeremiah, Daniel, Joel, etc.

Those who follow this false concept of a peace agreement then fall into the further trap of Satan, who deceives all whom he can with the One World concept of harmony that is contrary to the Jews and Christians. The New Age "Plan" calls for the death of all Jews and Christians, accusing them of having an "Armageddon complex" and therefore being warlike instead of calling for One World Utopian "peace."

Satan even carries his deceitfulness a step further by pointing out that Jesus said, "In the world ye shall have tribulation."[1] Don't fall for his lies! Jesus did say, "In the world ye shall have tribulation," but in the other half of that same verse, He said, "but be of good cheer; I have overcome the world!"

Jesus not only overcame the world and its law of sin and death, but He also overcame Satan. Jesus said of him in John 10:10, "The thief cometh not but to steal and to kill and to destroy: I am come that they might have life, and that they might have it more abundantly." And again, it is written in I John 3:8, "For this purpose the Son of God was manifested, THAT HE MIGHT DESTROY THE WORKS OF THE DEVIL."

Let us follow the true meaning of the prophecies and the promises of God in the Bible, comparing Scripture with Scripture to verify those prophecies.

THE REAL COVENANT WITH ISRAEL

The actual biblical statement in Dan. 9:27 is:

> And he shall *confirm* the covenant with many for one week; and in the midst of the week he shall cause the sacrifice and the oblation to cease...

The covenant referred to reveals two primary factors. He, (the "prince who shall come," the beast, the so-called antichrist, the king of the Revived Roman Empire of the end time) is to "confirm the covenant" with "many," which can only refer to the many people that now have returned to the land of Israel and have become the State of Israel. The king is to "confirm" the covenant with Israel for one week of years (7 years); and "in the midst of the week" he is to repudiate that covenant and shall, as a result, "cause the sacrifice and the oblation to cease."

1. John 16:33

THE REAL KING

Before considering the covenant and its meaning, it is vital that you have an understanding of the deeper meaning of "the king" and of his source of power. For this, we turn to a short exposition of the first verses of chapter 13 of the Book of Revelation. John writes:

> And I stood upon the sand of the sea, and saw a beast rise up out of the sea (the sea of the nations of the earth), having seven heads and ten horns, and upon his horns ten crowns, and upon his heads the name of blasphemy.[2]

The beast represented here is a composite of the seven Gentile powers that God allowed to rule over the city of Jerusalem during "the times of the Gentiles,"[3] namely: Babylon, Media, Persia, Egypt, Greece, Rome and the Revived Roman Empire. The ten crowns on the ten horns are defined in Dan. 7:7,8 and 24. Verse 8 reads,

> I considered the horns, and, behold, there came up among them another little horn, before whom there were three of the first horns plucked up by the roots: and behold, in this horn were the eyes of a man, and a mouth speaking great things.

Dan. 7:7 states that this last beastly head is "diverse from all the beasts that were before it; AND IT HAD TEN HORNS." And then verse 8 goes on to say that ANOTHER LITTLE HORN comes up – "having eyes like the eyes of a man, and a mouth speaking great things." In other words, this king of the eleventh nation to join the European Community is the designated king that is to be given his unusual powers by the Devil, Lucifer, Satan, the dragon:

2. Rev. 13:1   3. Luke 21:24

And the dragon gave him his power, and his seat, and great authority.[4]

The Antichrist King is to be given far greater power than he now possesses, for he is to be given "great authority" by the dragon of the skies - Lucifer. He is to receive some of Lucifer's Satanic power!

WHEN?

Not now. It is withheld from him now by the power of God resident in the body of believers - the church. It will be only AFTER the Rapture of the Church that he can come into his end time authority.

The verifying scripture references are in II Thessalonians, chapter two. Paul, in writing to the Thessalonian Christians said,

> Remember ye not, that when I was yet with you, I told you these things? And now ye know what (who it is that) withholdeth that he might be revealed IN HIS TIME.
>
> For the mystery of iniquity doth already work (the spirit of Antichrist already is in the world[5]): only he who now letteth (hinders) will hinder, until he be taken out of the way.[6]

By definition: "He who now hinders until he be taken out of the way" refers to the Body of Christ (the believing Christians) as specified in Col. 1:18, which reads, "And He (Jesus Christ our Lord) is the head of the body, THE CHURCH, who is the beginning, the firstborn from the dead."

As Jesus rose from the dead, even so shall we also be raised up:

4. Rev. 13:2   5. I John 4:3   6. II Thess. 2:7

For the Lord himself shall descend from heaven with a shout, with the voice of the archangel, and with the trump of God: and the dead in Christ shall rise first: then we which are alive and remain (at that moment) shall be caught up together with them in the clouds to meet the Lord in the air: and so shall we ever be with the Lord.[7]

II Thess. 2:8 then picks up the scenario:

And THEN shall that Wicked (One) be revealed, whom the Lord (ultimately) shall consume with the spirit of His mouth, and shall destroy with the bright-ness of His coming (in power per Rev. 19): even him, whose coming is after the working of Satan with all power and signs and lying wonders, and with all deceivableness of unrighteousness in them that perish, because they received not the love of the truth (of the Gospel), that they might be saved.

And for this cause God shall send them strong delu-sion, that they should believe a lie: that they all might be damned, who believed not the truth, but had plea-sure in unrighteousness.

While we Christians still are in the world and are proclaiming the Gospel of salvation by grace through faith in Jesus Christ, being cleansed by His blood and being redeemed by the power of His resurrection; the Devil's Antichrist king is held in check, is "hindered" from being revealed as the head of the Revived Roman Empire. He may anticipate his destiny, but he still has no legal authority beyond his own country from the Pope or from any other Western European power.

When we are "caught up" to be with the Lord, however, at the Rapture of the Church, THEN the hindering factor of

7. I Thess. 4:16, 17

the Body of Christ is removed to the glories of heaven, and THEN that Wicked One can and will march onto the world scene "with all power and signs and lying wonders, and with all deceivableness."[8]

As a result of the display of his demonic powers, he then will be acclaimed by the Western European nations of the Revived Roman Empire as their king, their leader, their "Emperor" in fulfillment of the prophecy of Rev. 17:12 and 13, which reads,

> And the ten horns which thou sawest are ten kings, which have received no kingdom as yet: but receive power as kings one hour with the beast. These have one mind, and shall give their power and strength unto the beast.

Having received their approval and appointment and authority as head of the European Union, he THEN will have the capacity to "uproot" three of the *original* members, leaving seven of them, plus his own country of Spain and plus Portugal and, by then, Austria, constituting then the final 10 nation Revised and Revived Roman Empire of the end time.

HIS ANTICIPATION

Does the King have any idea of that which lies ahead of him? Does he have any indication of his ultimate destiny? Is there any Satanic influence in his background or his actions? Does he anticipate his coming "power" and the source of that power?

Numerous writings indicate that the Bourbons of France and of Spain were much involved in the occult practices of the Druids. Especially is it declared that they were deeply

---

8. II Thess. 2:9, 10

steeped in the Black Serpent Cult which often is referred to as the "Death Cult," the serpent alluding to the dragon of the skies — Lucifer.

"THE DRAGON" AT THE OLYMPICS

That the occult influences continue today is very evident by the tremendously demonic display in the closing exercises of the 25th Olympiad in Barcelona, Spain on August 9, 1992. With the full knowledge of, and even under the direction of King Juan Carlos, who had to approve all actions therein, the occult, including the Black Serpent Cult, was flamboyantly displayed.

The October issue of American Information Newsletter, quoting from "Dancing Devils at the Olympics," a Pro Family Forum pamphlet, stated:

> The closing spectacle at the Olympic games this past summer in Barcelona, Spain, was an exercise in demonic/pagan symbolism which ended with the mating of a BLACK SERPENT and the Greek goddess of love and fertility, the multi-breasted Artemis who then gave birth to the "Great Dragon," the head of which rose 75 feet above the top of the stadium. The alleged theme of the pageant was the birth of the world in fire and it was represented by "250 'happy' devils... who began the 'festival of fire.' Giant wooden structures including two caped figures of Satan and grinning goat's head, were set ablaze and constantly moved through the cavorting devils. A group of devils, *one dressed in the robes of a king,* danced frenziedly around a fiery maypole... Weird tones, underlaid with constant 'jungle' drumming, were sporadically joined by eerie wails, long sighs and howling."

> Occult symbols were everywhere. Well represented were the Baphomet (goat's head of witchcraft), the

pentagram or "devil's star," the maypole, which is an ancient pagan phallic symbol, and demonic faces well endowed with horns. As expected, television network commentators were "awed" by the spectacle and competed with one another to compliment its "creativity." At times, the audience joined the celebration, swaying to the demonic music with arms outstretched to heaven.

Such was the description, and Mrs. Taylor and I watched it on international television in our home, hardly believing that it actually was happening, and feeling a great sense of demonic influence. Several of our friends said that they turned it off, for it was "too heavy" in occultism for them. Later, a friend of this *Today In Bible Prophecy* ministry wrote to us stating that she was there at the stadium when this took place and had an excellent view of it, for she had acquaintance with the Juan Carlos family. She stated that when it became too weird, she and her group walked past the King's special box, excusing themselves from the spectacle. Her further statement to me was that Prince Felipe, who sat just behind King Juan Carlos, got up and stated that he also was leaving. To which Juan Carlos snapped, "You can't leave now," only to get the reply "Just watch me." Even the prince evidently was disgusted by it all, showing disdain for the Satanic implications and displays. But not one bit of it could have occurred without the full approval of, if not the design of, King Juan Carlos. Does he anticipate the powers of the Devil, which Rev. 13:2 says will be imparted?

FURTHER EVIDENCE

In 1987, New Ager Ruth Montgomery, while being interviewed by a representative of *New Age Journal,* was asked, "When was the last time you did the automatic writing? Her reply was quite revealing:

The day before yesterday. This darling Mrs. Kluge and her husband were going to visit King Juan Carlos of Spain for the weekend, and she was pleading with me to ask something about Juan Carlos because she said he was getting interested (in psychic things). And I thought, now that could be helpful for a ruler, and so I did ask (the spirits) about him.

"And what did they say?"

I don't think I had better tell because it's too personal, but it was awfully good.

They said he is going to make some very wise decisions within the next decade that will not only help prepare his people, but Europe, too.

Question: Prepare for the shift?

Answer: Yes.

My friends, in New Age parlance, "the shift" refers to the great moment in history when they expect life on Mother Earth will "shift" to the Utopian Age of Aquarius when their people will take over the events of Earth, all opposition will be quelled, and there will be harmony on Earth because the opposing people (Christians and Jews and any who do not follow their Messiah Maitreya or the Space Brothers and Masters of Wisdom) will all be transferred to "another dimension".

For verification, David Spangler's book, *Revelation, the Birth of a New Age,* published in 1975, reports that they will not really be killing those of us who can't go along with their "christ," but will be sending us to another dimension other than physical reincarnation, to another vibration "where we'll be happier." In another of his books, *Reflections on the Christ,* he wrote: "The true light of Lucifer cannot be seen through sorrow, through darkness, through rejection. The true light of this great being can only be recognized when one's own eyes can see what is the true light of the Christ...The light of the inner sun, LUCIFER, works within each of us to bring us to wholeness as we move into a new age"; adding, "Lucifer comes to give us this final gift of wholeness. If we accept it, then he is free and we are free. That is the Luciferian initiation ," stating that we all had to take it if we wished to enter the New Age.

Alice Bailey, another New Ager, on page 107 of her book *The Ruler of Humanity,* wrote: "The ruler is LUCIFER, son of the morning." Part of that title is correct, for it is taken from Isaiah 14:12-15, quote,

> How art thou fallen from heaven, O Lucifer, son of the morning! how art thou cut down to the ground, which didst weaken the nations!
>
> For thou hast said in thine heart, *I will* ascend into heaven, *I will* exalt my throne above the stars of God: *I will* sit also upon the mount of the congregation, in the sides of the north:
>
> *I will* ascend above the heights of the clouds; *I will be like the most High.* (Such arrogance and rebellion against the Lord God!)
>
> YET THOU SHALT BE BROUGHT DOWN TO HELL, TO THE SIDES OF THE PIT.

In similar rebellion against our God and His Christ who is our Redeemer, Alice Bailey, David Spangler, Benjamin Creme, Lord Maitreya and their followers want to "do it their way," standing with Lucifer regardless of the consequences decreed by God Almighty. They apparently have believed the lies of Lucifer, who claims to have loomed above God as illustrated by the following quote from *MACKEY'S REVISED HISTORY OF FREEMASONRY* by Robert Ingham Clegg, 33°, volume seven, page 2116:

> In the Darkness is the genetrix, in the Light is the wisdom: the first imaged by devils, the other by angels, as a similitude of the whole eternal being, to speak as a

creature. AND LUCIFER, IMAGING BEYOND THE MEEKNESS OF THE TRINITY, kindled in himself the matrix of Fire, and that of nature, becoming corporeal, then was the second form of the matrix, *viz*, the meekness of the substantiality enkindled, whence water originated, out of which was made an heaven to captivate the fire, and of that Fire and Water came the Stars.

Thusly saying in essence, that Lucifer superceded the Trinity, generated Fire from within himself, via which he created Water, and of the Fire and the Water of himself created the heavens and the earth. Such arrogance! No wonder that God threw him out of heaven! Even Jesus stated "I beheld Satan as lightning fall from heaven."[9]

Beware of any Lodge or religion that does not exalt the Lord Jesus. If they worship "God," be sure that it is not Lucifer, who presents himself as the Light or as The Great Architect of the Universe (TGAOTU) that makes the lowly creature greater than the Creator God Almighty. Ezek. 28:14, 15 states, "Thou art the anointed cherub that covereth; and I have set thee so... Thou wast perfect in thy ways from the day that THOU WAST CREATED, till iniquity was found in thee... and thou hast sinned: THEREFORE I WILL CAST THEE AS PROFANE OUT OF THE MOUNTAIN OF GOD: AND I WILL DESTROY THEE, O COVERING CHERUB from the midst of the stones of fire." Verse 18 goes on to say, "Therefore will I bring forth a fire from the midst of thee, it shall devour thee, and I will bring thee to ashes upon the earth in the sight of all them that behold thee" (ultimately, when Rev. 20:10 is fulfilled after the millennial rule of Christ on Earth and the final rebellion of the Devil has been defeated "And the devil that deceived them was cast into the lake of fire and brimstone, where the beast and false prophet

9. Luke 10:18

are, and SHALL BE TORMENTED DAY AND NIGHT FOR
EVER AND EVER" for all the sickness and sorrow and
deaths that he has perpetrated upon humanity from the days
of Adam, for even Ezek. 28: 13 says, "Thou hast been in
Eden the garden of God.") This enemy of mankind was
called by Jesus a liar: saying even to the unbelieving
Pharisees in John 8:44,

> Ye are of your father the devil, and the lusts of your
> father ye will do. He was a murderer from the begin-
> ning (causing the death of Abel), and abode not in the
> truth, because there is no truth in him. When he
> speaketh a lie, he speaketh of his own, for he is a liar,
> and the father of it.

So clever a liar is Lucifer-Satan, that he even usurps the
biblical covenant of Daniel 9:27 and turns it to his own evil
designs, duping millions of people worldwide into following
after his call for "Peace" by compromises, mysticism and
rituals including free love unhampered by Judeo-Christian
inhibitions or regulations.. According to him, let peace
prevail at any cost and all can live free as hippies in a
Utopian society. Concerning this, the Bible decrees:

> There is a way that seemeth right unto a man, but
> the end thereof are the ways of death.[10]

By contrast, Jesus said, "I am come that ye might have life,
and have it more abundantly." Follow the way of Jesus, for
He loves you and wants only the best for you. "Believe on the
Lord Jesus Christ, and you shall be saved" is the sure promise
of God.

Do not be deceived, therefore, by the lies of Lucifer and do
not be destroyed by the evil devices of his Satanic tempta-

10. Prov. 14:12

tions. "Trust in the Lord with all thine heart... in all your ways acknowledge Him, and He shall direct your paths." This also is the promise of God.

FROM DAN OF ISRAEL?

It is recorded in Gen. 49:17 that when Jacob declared his final blessings, promises and pronouncements on his twelve sons, the children of Israel, he said of Dan:

> Dan shall be a serpent by the way, an adder in the path, that biteth the horse heels, so that his rider shall fall backward.

Years later, when the ten northern tribes departed from the kingdom of Judah after the death of Solomon, they were led by Jeroboam, the son of Nebat, who was an idol worshipper. As their king, he made the following determination:

> If this people go up to do sacrifice in the house of the Lord at Jerusalem, then shall the heart of this people turn again unto their lord, even unto Rehoboam king of Judah, and they shall kill me, and go again to Rehoboam king of Judah.
>
> Whereupon the king took counsel, and made two calves of gold, and said to them, It is too much for you to go up to Jerusalem: behold thy gods, O Israel, which brought thee up out of the land of Egypt.
>
> And he set the one in Bethel, and the other put he in Dan.
>
> And this thing became a sin: for the people went to worship before the one, even unto Dan.[11]

Almost all of the kings of the northern tribes of Israel followed in the way of Jeroboam, serving idols, even as it was said of King Baasha in I kings 16:34,

11. I Kings 12:26-30

> And he did evil in the sight of the Lord, and walked
> in the way of Jeroboam, and in his sin wherewith he
> made Israel to sin.

Finally, it became too much, and God's judgment fell on
the ten tribes of Israel:

> Then the king of Assyria came up throughout all the
> land, and went up to Samaria, and besieged it three
> years.
> In the ninth year of Hoshea;the king of Assyria took
> Samaria, and carried Israel away into Assyria, and
> placed them...in the cities of the Medes.
> For so it was that the children of Israel had sinned
> against the Lord their God, which had brought them
> up out of the land of Egypt, from under the hand of
> Pharaoh king of Egypt, and had feared other gods.
> For they served idols, whereof the Lord had said
> unto them, Ye shall not do this thing.[12]

In Amos 9:9, God declares, "Lo, I will command, and I will
sift the house of Israel among all nations, like as corn is sifted
in a sieve, yet shall not the least grain fall upon the earth."

ISRAEL'S DISPERSAL

Historians record that in the reign of Esarhaddon, king of
Assyria, the conquered people of Israel were called Gimira.
The Grecians, recording the same events, referred to them as
"Kimmerioi," which we translate into English as
"Cimmerian."

About 600 B.C., the Lydians drove the Gimira, or
Cimmerians, out of Asia Minor. They settled in the
Carpathian regions west of the Black Sea. Those who had

---

12. II Kings 17:5-7, 12

settled in the Armenian region, however, moved further north through the Dariel Pass into the steppes of south Russia where they became known by the name "Scythians."

As they rounded the Black Sea, they joined with others of the Cimmerians that had been driven out of Lydia (Turkey) into Greece and into the Balkan region at the mouth of the Danube River.

Many biblical historians believe it was primarily the descendants of the tribe of Dan who moved on up the Danube River, and even on to Danzig. In the Budapest to Vienna regions, of them came the line of the Hapsburgs and emporers of the Austrian and the Holy Roman empires. Others of the Cimmerians migrated further west, becoming known as Cimbri or Celts. They invaded northern Italy and moved on into Gaul, which today is modern France, joining with others to head the Bourbon dynasties of Luxembourg and The Netherlands.

Migrating further south, some crossed the Pyrenees Mountains into Spain and were called Iberians, which is the Gaelic name for Hebrews. A strong Jewish element developed there during Spain's golden years, and it was there that the Rambam, Maimonides, taught Jewish law and tradition.

THE HAPSBURG CONNECTION

After the fall of the Roman Empire in A.D. 476, the primary rule gradually was usurped by the Popes of the Roman Catholic Church. By A.D. 800, Charlemagne, king of the Franks, was crowned in Rome by Pope Leo III as Emporer of the West. His biographer, Einhard, stated: "He vanquished and made tributary all the wild and barbarous tribes dwelling in Germany between the Rhine and the Vistula, the ocean and the Danube."

Conquests, religious pressures and intermarriages produced monarchs and dynasties over the centuries: the

Hapsburgs in Germany and Austria, the Bourbons of France and Spain and the Anglo-Saxons of the British Isles being among the most prominent.

BRIEF LINEAGE OF KING JUAN CARLOS I

In *World Events Relating to the Bible,* I wrote, "He is a direct descendent of Louis XIV of the Bourbon dynasty of France and also of the Hapsburgs of Austria and Germany dating back to the Holy Roman Empire. Juan, the only son of Ferdinand and Isabella of Spain married Maximillian's daughter, Margaret, linking Castile and Aragon of Spain with Austria. At the death of Maximillian I of Hapsburg, his grandson Charles became king of Germany and in February, 1530, Pope Clement crowned Charles "Holy Roman Emperor Charles V." He was the last "Holy Roman Emperor" to be crowned by a Pope, and this same Charles V of Austria was also Charles I of Spain.

King Juan Carlos I was born in Rome, Italy January 5, 1938.

His full name is Juan Carlos Alfonso Victor Maria de Borbon y Borbon, born of the son of HRH Don Juan de Borbon y Battenberg, Count of Barcelona, HRH Dona Maria de las Mercedes de Borbon y Orleans. He is the grandson of King Alfonso XIII and Queen Victoria Eugenia of Spain and great, great grandson of the renowned Queen Victoria of Great Britain.

On May 14, 1962, Prince Juan Carlos married Sofia, the sister of exiled King Constantine of Greece. In her lineage are 2 German emperors, 8 kings of Denmark, 5 kings of Sweden, 7 Czars of Russia, 1 king and 1 queen of Norway, 1 queen of England and 5 kings of Greece. Indeed, if King Juan Carlos I of Spain is eventually crowned by a Pope of Rome, he could most certainly become the emperor the Revived Roman Empire!

FURTHER EVIDENCE

A report in HOLA Magazine in 1972 stated that "Prince Juan Carlos of Spain took second place in the pre-Olympic 'sailing races' in Kiel, Germany. The event took place upon the North Sea, and the Prince of Spain sailed to second place in a craft entitled 'THE DRAGON.' The races were conducted under the auspices of the pre-Olympic trials, under the banner of 'the Munich games.'"

In another report shortly after Juan Carlos became King of Spain it is stated that he said, "I like the power of flying." He had just tested the U.S. F-18 jet, and stated: "This plane will satisfy our aerial needs." Spanish Air Force Colonel "Ostos" stated that "The king performs perfect aerobatics."

Still another source says, "The king's love for speed is frightening!"

A graduate of Spain's Military Academy, its Naval Academy and also of its Air Force Academy, King Juan Carlos is highly qualified by land, by sea or by air to become Spain's (and soon Europe's) mighty military leader. If, as "King of Jerusalem, DEFENDER of Catholic Holy Land interests," he could be seen coming on the *world* scene as the biblical rider on "the white horse" of Rev. 6:2, right after the Rapture of the Church as evidenced in Rev. 5:9, and will be seen to go forth "conquering and to conquer." It will be to defend Israel when the "red" Soviets and Muslim forces attack Jerusalem soon after the "peace talks" fail to satisfy the Arab demands for the eastern half of Jerusalem, including the Temple Mount, for their capital of their hoped-for State of Palestine (which they shall never have). Rev. 6:4 states that they shall have "power to take peace from the earth, and that they should kill one another," verse 8 stating that one-fourth of mankind (left on earth after the Rapture) shall be killed. Ezek. 39:12 says it will take the Israelis seven months to bury the dead enemies that will have come against them.

Is all of this getting ready to happen? Let us now consider the prophesied and now formulated JERUSALEM COVENANT that declares uniquivically that Jerusalem is and shall be for ever the capitol of the State of Israel.

THE JERUSALEM COVENANT

By way of background, Abraham paid tithes to Melchizadek, the priest of God, at Salem. By 1000 B.C., King David had conquered Jerusalem (Salem) from the Jebusites and made it the capital of the nation of Israel.

Jerusalem was later lost to the Babylonians in 586 B.C., but rebuilt and reinhabited by the Jewish people under Ezra and Nehemiah, continuing until the city and its holy Temple were destroyed by the Romans in A.D. 70.

At the time of the joyous return from exile under Ezra and Nehemiah, the leaders and people of Israel made a covenant with Jerusalem, declaring their allegiance to God and concluding with the statement: *"And we will not forsake the house of our God"* as recorded in Nehemiah 9:38 and 10:39.

Israel was restored as a nation, in fulfillment of many Bible prophecies in May, 1948, but did not have the city of Jerusalem. That was won in the Six-Day War of 1967. Celebrating that day as JERUSALEM DAY 25 years later, on May 31, 1992, Yeshaya Barzel, Director General of the Ministry for Jerusalem Affairs called for a "worldwide celebration to reaffirm the indelible bond between the Jewish people and its eternal spiritual and cultural capitol." A special "JERUSALEM COVENANT" exemplifying the earlier Covenant was drafted, beautifully prepared, signed by 16 of Israel's top officials and sent to worldwide Jewish centers for the signatures of "many" dignitaries; then to be returned to Jerusalem to be presented to the President of Israel on JERUSALEM DAY (of the Jewish calendar), May 19, 1993.

The prophecy in Daniel 9:27 contains the key prophecy that the end-time king of the revived Roman empire

"SHALL CONFIRM THE COVENANT WITH MANY" (Israelis) for one week of years, which is interpreted by virtually all Bible scholars as being the physical act that will start the seven-year "time of Jacob's trouble," better known as the Tribulation Period.

Note that there absolutely is no mention of this being a "peace agreement" that so many prophecy men make it out to be. Everyone naturally wants "peace and safety," but that is not the factor nor the issue here in Dan. 9: 27. Also, it does *not* say that he will "make" a treaty with Israel, let alone with its militant Arab and Islamic enemies. The actual Bible declaration is that *(when* he has been given his full authority as king of the revived Roman empire by the leaders thereof) "HE SHALL *CONFIRM* THE COVENANT," meaning that he will add his signature of confirmation and approval to an already established covenant; and it shall be with "many." By design and purpose, the JERUSALEM COVENANT now has been circulated among the Jewish leaders of the nations of the world for one year and has been returned to the capital of Israel, Jerusalem. It thereby already has the signatures of approval by "many" Israelis. NOW IT CAN BE CONFIRMED "WITH MANY!"

THE MEANING OF THE CONFIRMATION

I submit to you that THIS IS THE COVENANT prophesied by the Lord God by His prophet Daniel more than 2,500 years ago! It already has been signed by "many" and now is ready for the signature of CONFIRMATION by the "King of Jerusalem, defender of Catholic Holy Land interests," who is identified as King Juan Carlos of Spain, the king of the eleventh nation to join the Treaty of Rome (1957) European Community in fulfillment of Dan. 7:8 and 24.

Inasmuch as it is stated in 2 Thess. 2:7 and 8 that the end-time dictator king of the revived Roman empire can not receive his full authority and be revealed to the world as its leader until after "we" have been "caught up" in the clouds to meet the Lord in the air (1 Thess. 4:17) at the Rapture of the Church, for "THEN shall that Wicked (one) be revealed... even him whose coming is after the working of Satan with all power and signs and lying wonders" (2 Thess. 2:8,9), THE RAPTURE MUST BE NEAR!

WHEN?

Not knowing the exact moment, "for ye know neither the day nor the hour wherein the Son of man cometh" (Matt. 25:13), but seeing these mighty "signs of the times" being fulfilled before our eyes, it should make us to be "fervent in spirit, serving the Lord," as He commanded. This no longer can be called speculation, for the facts are all before us. Israel became a nation again 45 years ago, gained the city of Jerusalem in 1967 and now has issued its JERUSALEM COVENANT which states: "We love you, O Jerusalem... Our faithfulness to you we shall bequeath to our children after us. FOREVERMORE, OUR HOME SHALL BE WITH YOU."

The Muslims of the world will be furious and will despise it, wanting to destroy it and the nation that proclaims it. But they dare not to attack yet because of the Christian world's backing of the nation of Israel. When the Rapture of the Church takes place, however, and millions of believing Christians instantly disappear from this earth, they will believe the lies of the New Age Movement and feel that their time has come. Furthermore, when the "King of Jerusalem" steps forth from the Western European Community and signs his name to the JERUSALEM COVENANT, thusly guaranteeing it, their war against Israel will be with religious fury. In spite of all of their effort and of their Eastern European Muslim allies, they will be horribly defeated for it is prophesied in Isaiah 19, Ezekiel 38 and 39, Ezekiel 32 and elsewhere in the Scriptures that they "shall fall on the mountains of Israel."

God's Word will have its exact fulfillment in His exact time, and all of the preparations for these events taking place today indicate that it must be very, very soon.

IT HAPPENED AS DECLARED

May 29, 1993, Jerusalem Post: The 26th anniversary of Jerusalem's reunification was marked last Wednesday with massive marches and solemn memorial services throughout the capital.

The nation's leaders gathered at Ammunition Hill (in northern segment of Jerusalem) in the afternoon, reaffirming Israel's sovereignty over Jerusalem and expressing their hope for peace. Cabinet ministers, Ministers of the Knesset, Israel Defense Force and police brass were among the 1,500 attending the ceremony, which this year included THE SIGNING OF THE COVENANT OF JERUSALEM.

Seventy leaders of world Jewry gathered at Beit Hanassi to sign the covenant, meant to express the bond between Diaspora Jews and Jerusalem as the undivided capital of Israel. THE COVENANT — which was signed a year ago by Israeli leaders, and on Jerusalem Day by President Ezer Weizman — is based on biblical quotations and themes from the writings of the Sages, Jewish tradition and Israeli law.

Tens of thousands of people participated in a prayer service for Jerusalem at the Western Wall, sponsored by the Religious Affairs Ministry.

Jerusalem Covenant

Last of 7 illustrated gates and last paragraph,
plus original signatures on the Covenant

"**A**nd with all these understandings, we enter into this Covenant and write': We shall bind you to us forever; we shall bind you to us with faithfulness, with righteousness and justice, with steadfast love and compassion. We love you, O Jerusalem, with eternal love, with unbounded love, under siege and when liberated from the yoke of oppressors. We have been martyred for you; we have yearned for you, we have clung to you. Our faithfulness to you we shall bequeath to our children after us. Forevermore, our home shall be within you.

In certification of this covenant, we sign:

Speaker of the Knesset   Prime Minister   President State of Israel

Chief Rabbi (Sephardi)   Chief Rabbi (Ashkenazi)   President Supreme Court

Chairman Ministerial
Committee for Ceremony   Deputy Prime Minister   Deputy Prime Minister

Mayor of Jerusalem   Deputy Minister for
                            Jerusalem Affairs   Chairman World
                                                       Zionist Organization

Representative of Bereaved Families
for the Battles of Jerusalem   Chief of Staff Six Day War   Deputy President
                                                                          Supreme Court

                            Minister for Education and Culture

Chapter Six

THE POPES AND THE KING

Much could be said about the many Popes of Rome, but their political power seemed to be exemplified the most by their appointments of the emperors of the Holy Roman Empire from the crowning of Charlemagne in A.D. 800 to the last Holy Roman Emperor Charles V in 1530. And this Charles V was also known as King Charles I of Spain.

Papal influence still is strong in predominantly Roman Catholic countries such as Spain. When King Alfonso XIII and Queen Victoria Eugenia were exiled from Spain in 1931 because Spain became a Republic, he and Queen Eugenia moved to Rome, taking with them Prince Don Juan and his new wife, Princess Dona Maria de las Mercedes de Borbon y Orleans. While in Rome, Princess Mercedes gave birth to Juan Carlos on Jan. 5, 1938.

Knowing that Prince Don Carlos truly wanted to become the next king of Spain, Queen Victoria Eugenia appealed to Pope Pius XII (Pacelli) to designate her grandson, Juan Carlos, to become the king-designate instead of Communist-leaning Prince Don Carlos. Don Carlos objected, but to no avail.

Ten years later, in 1948, the same year that Israel became a nation again after 2,500 years of exile, Don Juan again appealed to Pope Pius XII to designate him to become the next king of Spain. The Pope refused him the request, and so Don Carlos sent his son, Juan Carlos to Madrid to be trained by Generalissimo Francisco Franco to become the next king. He remained under the care and extensive training of Franco for the next 27 years. As stated in Dan. 9:26, he truly became "the prince who shall come."

History records that on July 23, 1969, Generalissimo Francisco Franco stood before a full session of the Spanish Cortes (Parliament) and declared:

> "The relief of the Chief of State is a normal act imposed by man's mortality. Conscious of my responsibility before God and history, I have decided to recommend Prince Juan Carlos de Borbon y Borbon as my successor."

In November, 1975, Gen. Franco passed from this life, and Prince Juan Carlos became King Juan Carlos I, King of Spain.

THE CORONATION OF THE KING

Nov. 27, 1975, Los Angeles Herald and Examiner: MADRID, Spain (AP) Flanked by European royalty and three Common Market presidents, King Juan Carlos received the highest blessing of the Roman Catholic Church and the cheers of thousands of countrymen as Spain paid homage to its new leader.

Shouts of "Long Live Spain" and "Long Live the King" greeted the 37-year old monarch and his wife, Queen Sofia, as they rode through the capital's streets to Mass at the 16th century Church of Los Jeronimos ahead of a full military parade.

Inside the church, the biggest gathering (from 68 countries) of foreign dignitaries in Spain's history watched as the church's political voice, Vincente Cardinal Enrique y Tarancon, the liberal archbishop of Madrid, celebrated Mass of the Holy Spirit...

Seated on the front rows were President Valery Giscard d'Estain of France, West German President Walter Scheel and Irish President Cearbhail Odalaigh. Scheel was flanked by the Duke of Edinburgh, Britain's representative, and Prince Rainier of Monaco. U.S. Vice President Nelson Rockefeller was one row back.

KING JUAN CARLOS IN ROME

Five years after his coronation as king, but five years before Spain became a member of the European Community, the King and Queen of Spain were invited to Rome, Italy.

> *June, 1981, SPAIN:* King Juan Carlos and Queen Sofia paid a three-day official visit to Italy as the guests of the president, Sandro Pertini. It is the first time in 58 years that a Spanish Head of State has visited Italy. The last to do so was King Alfonso in 1923.
>
> At the banquet offered to Their Majesties, Sgr. Sandro Pertini said that Spain's entry into the EC has been termed indispensable in order to accomplish the construction of Europe...
>
> In his reply to the Italian president, the King said: "I have come here with the feeling of returning to the sources, to the centre of a culture which irradiates our own, to the beloved city where I was born. *The peace and future of the world are also at stake here...*"

HIS AUDIENCE WITH THE POPE

Before returning to Madrid, Their Majesties the King and Queen were received at a special audience by Pope John Paul II. The photograph is of the King kissing the Papal ring while Queen Sofia looks on. Her Majesty was dressed in white, a privilege granted to Catholic queens. His Holiness had a friendly chat with the King and Queen.

King Juan Carlos of Spain became an honorary citizen of Rome during a ceremony at the city council chamber. The King was born in Rome.

THE DEMISE OF DON JUAN

Apr. 4, 1993, Reuters: Don Juan de Borbon y Battenburg, father of Spain's King Juan Carlos never ruled, but was buried in the Panteon de los Reyes alongside most of Spain's monarchs. He died April 1, 1993.

THE KING AND THE POPE

King Juan Carlos and the Spanish people have felt honored by numerous visits by Pope John Paul II to Spain. As "King of Jerusalem," Juan Carlos also must have a strong desire to see the Pope visit the Holy City of Jerusalem. It seems logical, and the leaders of Israel have sought for it, Foreign Minister Peres having repeatedly invited the Pope to Jerusalem. He was expected to come in 1992, or at least by 1993. A news article in *Jerusalem Post,* however, sheds a revealing light on the subject.

> *Nov. 7, 1992, Jerusalem Post:* The prospect of an official papal visit to Israel in the near future dimmed considerably last week, following initial reports that Pope John Paul II had accepted an invitation from Foreign Minister Shimon Peres.
>
> A message sent to Church officials and Roman Catholic leaders in the region, apparently aimed at clarifying the outcome of the meeting between the pope and Peres, made no mention of officially accepting the invitation, or a date for a proposed visit.
>
> Instead, the thrust of the message reiterated the Vatican's press communique, which spoke only of the Pope's "deep desire" to make "a pilgrimage" one day to the Holy Land. A later announcement said the pope wished only to come as a pilgrim. That meant, said Uri Mor, director of the Religious Affairs Ministry department for Christian communities, that even if the pontiff did come, *it would not be on an official visit.*

The initial reports that Pope John Paul II had accepted Peres's invitation to visit brought angry reactions from some Arab and Islamic countries, which charged that such a visit would be tantamount to accepting Israeli sovereignty over Jerusalem... Yasser Arafat said that according to information in his possession, the pope would NOT visit Jerusalem in the near future.

THE BACKGROUND

As researched by Mr. Dean Curcio and verified through Jack Chick Publications,[1] the reason for the refusal goes back many centuries.

About 610 A.D., Muhammed of Arabia claimed that he had a vision from Allah (Islamic term for God) who showed him a majestic being whom he called Gabriel, who reportedly said, "You are the messenger of Allah." Not long thereafter, Muhammed declared that Gabriel awakened him one night and led him to a heavenly type of animal with wings named "Buraq." When he mounted "Buraq" he reputedly was flown to the Jewish temple mount in Jerusalem, from which he was carried to heaven where he claimed that he received the creed of Islam and instructions for five daily prayers to Allah.[2]

His claim of going to heaven (and back) from Jerusalem led to the Arab claim of Jerusalem as the third holy city of Islam, after Mecca and Medina. Muhammed moved his center of action from Mecca in 622 A.D. It was from Medina that he began his raids on the "Razzias," the caravans, and on Jewish settlements and ultimately throughout the Middle East.

1. Chick Publications, P.O. Box 662, Chino, CA 91708-0662
2. Muhammed, by Lings, Inter Traditionals, Ltd. NY

In 630 A.D., history tells us that Muhammed, with an army by then of over 10,000 men, marched on Mecca. The leaders of the city came out and yielded to him, and he won the city to and for Islam.

Roman Catholic leaders at this point became alarmed and concerned, and they sent teachers to Muhammed; and he became an ardent follower of the writings of Saint Augustine. He also was told by the Catholics that the Jews were the enemies of the church and thusly of his own teachings. He then formed an unholy alliance with the Roman Catholics, avowing three things: (1) They both would eliminate the Jews and evangelical Christians (non-Roman Catholic) as infidels: (2) In exchange for heavy financing for his armies, Muhammed would protect the Augustinian monks and Roman Catholics: (3) Muhammed would conquer Jerusalem for "His Holiness" in the Vatican.

In time, the power of Islam spread across North Africa and into Spain and also through Turkey and Greece into Eastern Europe, and Jerusalem was in Muslim hands. Another agreement was made that Muslims could build mosques in Catholic countries as long as Roman Catholicism could flourish in Arab countries. Their agreement apparently held, for Roman Catholics were not slaughtered as were the Jews and Bible-believing Christians.

When the Pope asked for Jerusalem, however, the Muslim generals refused, saying that they had won it and that one of their great leaders, Omar Ibn Al-Khattab had built the Dome of the Rock memorial to Ishmael and to Muhammed there, and it was to be an Islamic city for ever.

20TH CENTURY TURN OF EVENTS

At the turn of the century, Spain's Roman Catholic King Alfonso XIII had severe problems. Quoting from Collier's Encyclopedia, page 327,

The normal ills of Spanish life were complicated by
the development of radicalism and the growth of the
home rule idea, especially in Catalonia. In 1923,
Alfonso disavowed the existing Government and with
the army created the dictatorship of Gen. Rivera...
Unable to withstand the demands for change, the
Government consented to hold elections in 1931.

"The results were so strongly pro-republican that
Alfonso left the country. The Spanish Republic was
thereupon proclaimed with Nicito Alcala Zamora,
President."

The Vatican considered this to be a revolt against
Roman Catholic Alfonso and reportedly called on Islamic
leaders for help to break the new Spanish government. The
Spanish Civil War resulted as Generalissimo Francisco
Franco led a largely Muslim army from Morocco to the
Canary Islands and then to the Spanish mainland. To hide
the real reason, this civil war was acclaimed to be a holy
war against Communism, when in reality "the Spaniards
watched in shock as Cardinal Pedro Segura led the Islamic
army in slaughtering unfaithful Roman Catholic men,
women and children without mercy. About four million
Muslim troops occupied Spain as the protectors of the
Roman Catholic faith. Islam had paid her debt (for
refusing Jerusalem)."[3]

SECRET ARAB-VATICAN AGREEMENT

Arab willingness to fight for the Roman Catholic cause in
Spain, however, came with a price. The Muslims agreed to
help the Vatican IF the Pope NEVER would recognize any
state of Israel that might come into existence. The Pope

3. Chick Publications, Chino, CA

agreed, and to this day the Vatican has never officially recognized Israel as a nation. The status of Jerusalem, therefore, has remained in limbo and can only be changed officially when the Muslim armies and those of their Eastern European allies have been defeated in the great war of the (near) future prophesied in Isa. 19:13-17, which is the same war as that of Ezekiel 38 and 39 and of Rev. 6:4-8 that is to occur right AFTER the Rapture of the believers in Christ into the glories of heaven.

TODAY'S REJECTION BY THE VATICAN

God's perfect time not as yet having come to climax, the Arab-Vatican agreement still stands, as evidenced by the following news item, as previously stated in this chapter:

> *Nov. 7, 1992, Jerusalem Post:* ...One official in a Church institution with close ties to the Vatican said there had been no news about projected travel plans involving the Holy Land.
>
> An aide to Sabbah said that in the official communique from the Vatican, there was no message to the local church that any visit was in the offing.
>
> Uri Mor, director of the Religious Affairs Ministry department for Christian communities, pointed out that despite the announcement of Vatican Foreign Minister Monsignor Jean-Louis Tauran that Pope John Paul II is waiting for a formal invitation, the later announcement said the pope wished to come *as a pilgrim.* That meant, Mor said, that even *if the pontiff did come, it would not be on an official visit.*
>
> The initial reports that Pope John Paul II had accepted Peres's invitation to visit brought angry reactions from some Arab and Islamic countries, which charged that such a visit would be tantamount to accepting Israeli sovereignty over Jerusalem.

In an announcement from Tunis, PLO leader Yasser Arafat said that according to information in his possession, the pope would NOT visit Jerusalem in the near future.

And there you have the Arab-Vatican accord and its resulting stand-off. The Vatican still wants control of Jerusalem, but must bide its time, for the Muslims are not about to relinquish their claim to El Quds, "the holy place."

IN THE MEANTIME

King Juan Carlos of Spain is expanding his outreach.

April, 1992, Espana: The National Defense Committee met at the Zarzuela Palace, with H.M. King Juan Carlos presiding. This body is the Government's chief consultative organ on defense matters.

On the agenda for discussion was the National Defense Directive. The new Directive is to be applied in Spain over *the next eight years.*

For the first time Spain's Armed Forces are furnished with a project in which their tasks are to be extended beyond the area of internal defense. From now on the design of their field action is to be expanded so as to meet the commitments required by Spain's role on the *international scene,* in connection with NATO and the Western European Union (WEU).

The Directive also refers to the participation of the Armed Forces in humanitarian and *peace-keeping missions.* The defense project also deals with the responsibility of Spain in the many multidirectional risks which could arise as a result of the diversity of international tension, *including religious fundamentalism.*

This National Defense Directive, effective for the next 8 years, can easily cover the coming 7-year Tribulation Period, giving King Juan Carlos as Commander-in-Chief of the Spanish Armed Forces (and soon Europe's) full freedom to not only sign the JERUSALEM COVENANT, guaranteeing its protection, but also to act in its defense "in humanitarian and peace keeping missions" -including the protection of Israel from Islamic "religious fundamentalism."

The National Defense Committee, with H. M. the King presiding, discusses the new strategy following changes on the international scene as of 2/20/92 (in España, Apr. '92)

Chapter Seven

"AND BY PEACE – MANY"

Because the word "peace" is mentioned in Dan. 8:25 in relation to the coming end-time king, there are numerous Bible prophecy men who go overboard and try to declare that there will be no war at the beginning of the Tribulation Period, discarding the fact that many other Bible passages describe the war and the many nations that will be in it.

Some nations, however, will be taken over, absorbed and therefore overcome by peaceful contact. A perfect example of this is Spain's constant contact with and now domination of Latin America.

July 30, 1988, The Economist: In 1912, the pre-war peak year for emigration, 134,000 Spaniards settled in Latin America. Today an estimated 1.8 million Spanish passport-holders live in Latin America. Spain gives most Latin Americans the right to Spanish nationality - an arrangement that raises eyebrows in the EEC.

Spanish CATHOLIC involvement remains surprisingly strong. Over 85% of the Spanish nuns and priests who work abroad are in Latin America: 10,000 nuns, 7,000 friars and 1,000 diocesan priests, according to Spain's Episcopal Conference.

Opus Dei, a worldwide Catholic organization founded in Spain, is involved in everything from agricultural training to university education. Since the Spanish civil war, 40,000 Latin American post-graduation students (including Peru's President Alan Garcia) have studied in Spain on government grants, and some 5,000 are there now.

Spain's educational institutions are very formalistic and very susceptible to the Kingdom Now deceptions of the New Age Movement fostered to a great extent by Opus Dei, the movement through which King Juan Carlos received most of his early training, his confessor priest being of Opus Dei.

KING CARLOS AND LATIN AMERICA

King Juan Carlos of Spain has travelled more than any monarch in history. He has been to Latin America 18 times and now is tying those nations together in HIS Latin American Conference of Nations, working "assiduously" with Pres. Carlos Salinas of Mexico, according to *Wall Street Journal.*

> *September '91, ESPANA:* MADRID, Spain: For the first time in history, the Heads of State and Government of the 19 Spanish and Portuguese speaking countries of the American continent, plus Spain and Portugal, have come together to transform the complex of historic and cultural affinities by which we are linked into an instrument for unity, based on dialogue, cooperation and solidarity.
>
> The meeting took place in the Mexican city of Guadalajara on July 18th and 19th under the title of "lst Latin American Summit." At the close, the leaders of "The 21," in addition to signing a 24-point final declaration, decided to set themselves up as a permanent organic group which will be known as the Latin American Conference of Nations.
>
> It will meet at least once a year, with the next meeting in Madrid, *Spain.*

AN AMAZING DECLARATION
BY KING JUAN CARLOS

It was in one of his earlier visits to the nations of Latin America. Juan Carlos had come to Argentina, stopping at both Buenos Aires and Rosario. An official report is in *SPAIN*, published by the Diplomatic Information Office, Salvador 3, 28012 Madrid, Spain. In the May, 1985 issue, it states:

> The State visit of the King and Queen to the Argentine Republic ended with a brief trip to the Iguazu Falls. While in the Argentine, the King had a meeting with the President, Raul Alfonsin, made a speech to the Legislative Assembly and was acclaimed by crowds in Buenos Aires and Rosario. Throughout the five days of the visit, the King reaffirmed his commitment to the defense of liberties and human rights.
>
> Defense of democracy was the main theme of the King's speech to the Legislative Assembly during which he said, "NEVER MUST ANY IDEA OF THE STATE *OR ANY MESSIANIC DELIVERER* COME TO WREST FROM US OUR DIGNITY AS FREE MEN."
>
> The king assured his hearers that "by joining the European Community we are not cutting, but are taking with us to unite us to the European continent, the profound ties that bind us to Spanish America." The King also stated that his wish was "that Spain should be, without exception, the country of all Spaniards."

For Spain to be "the country of all Spaniards," is to be expected; but for King Juan Carlos to say, without any question being asked concerning the subject, that "NEVER MUST ANY IDEA OF THE STATE OR ANY MESSIANIC DELIVERER COME TO WREST FROM US OUR DIGNITY

AS FREE MEN," It implies that he is defying the very Lord God, who IS the Messiah and the Messianic Deliverer, and may therefore anticipate his future position of the Antichrist! We will know before long!

CANARY ISLANDS "A CROSSROADS"

June, '86, SPAIN: This year the Canary Island archipielago has been chosen for the celebration of the now traditional Armed Forces Day. The day's most outstanding features were a parade of army troops, in which 3,500 soldiers participated and a second air-sea parade in which 5,000 men, 14 warships and 50 aeroplanes took part. THE KING AND QUEEN OF SPAIN PRESIDED AT BOTH PARADES.

The splendor of the military Ceremony should be emphasized, with over 100,000 people present. King Juan Carlos referred to the Canaries as a crossroads between Europe and America, and stated he was "sure that you have accepted as on other occasions, the challenge of the new era in which we live, with Europe on one side and America on the other, in the middle of a world which requires the effort and efficiency of strong men."

UNITED KINGDOM
WELCOME AND PRAISE

June, '86, SPAIN: The visit of the king and queen has been called a success, having served to strengthen all nature of ties between the two nations. The honorary degree of doctor "honoris causa" was conferred on King Juan Carlos by the University of Oxford.

Furthermore The King was given the opportunity to address the British Parliament in a joint session of the two houses. The king's speech was greeted with a prolonged ovation and highly favorable comments by members of the British Parliament.

According to all observers this visit has been a complete success for Spanish and English diplomacy and A PERSONAL TRIUMPH FOR DON JUAN CARLOS who has been named "the best Spanish ambassador" by numerous newspapers.

JUAN CARLOS AND THE WORLD

King Juan Carlos and Queen Sofia have had invitations and acknowledgement of acceptance by doctorates being bestowed upon King Juan Carlos or his Queen by universities of many nations of the world. His personal charm and kingly stance has indeed won "many" by peaceful means. That is well exemplified by the President of Finland's statement in 1989 that "the King and Queen's visit to Finland brought out the excellent state of bilateral relations." Similar reports are on record from Nepal and New Zealand to Canada, Iceland, Europe and Latin America as well as from the Far East. In Thailand, King Carlos referred to the exploits of the Spanish seafarers in "an enterprise which culminated in the incorporation of America, together with Europe, Africa,Asia and the Pacific, IN A WORLD WHICH FOR THE FIRST TIME WAS ONE."[1] Yes, He is vitally interested in One World!

> *Nov. '91, Espana:* The visit by King Juan Carlos and Queen Sofia to the United States has made it clear that relations between Spain and the United States, which are not clouded by any kind of dispute, are in excellent state.
>
> The American Senate interrupted its session in order to extend an affectionate welcome to the King and

1. Jan. '88, SPAIN

Queen. The visit of Their Majesties the king and queen to the United States, with over thirty official engagements, also showed that King Juan Carlos and Queen Sofia are beyond all doubt the best ambassadors for today's Spain.

Nov, '91, Espana: "It is our aim to make Spain in 1992 a rendezvous for men and women from all over the world, a confluence of cultural and scientific contributions and sporting achievements, an area for reflection and plans *for our common future,*" His Majesty King Juan Carlos told the General Assembly of the United Nations on October 7th, when he recalled that in that year Spaniards would have "the signal responsibility" of hosting such outstanding events as the Barcelona Olympic Games, the World Exhibition in Seville and the 2nd Latin American Conference.

King Juan Carlos explained to the United Nations delegates the main outlines of Spain's policy regarding *the new international order.*

THE YEAR OF SPAIN

Jan. 6, 1992, TIME Mag.: For every Spaniard the arrival of 1992 is the culmination of a lengthy countdown. For this the long-heralded year of Spain, when the country will take center of the global stage and demonstrate its emergence as a modern democratic nation.

International attention has been captured by the confluence of high profile events. More importantly, *the end of 1992 marks Spain's fullfledged membership in the European Community.* (Ed. - Now officially in!)

1992, due to the efforts the country has made to improve its infrastructure, will not only be the year of Spain but *the first in a series of "years of Spain."*

"We invested for manana," said Jacinto Pellon, managing director of Expo '92, where Japan and the

United Kingdom each spent $70 million on their pavilions. The Expo itself, based on the theme "An Age of Discovery," has attracted 100 nations, 20 international organizations, 17 regions of Spain and seven corporate pavilions to enchant an anticipated 18-20 million visitors.

Expo represents the new Spain in the new Europe.

LOOKING FORWARD to His Reign as "KING OF THE WORLD"

King of Spain and Pres. of Israel at Synagogue in Madrid 3/31/92

Rabbi Blesses King Carlos in Ceremony of Reconciliation

Chapter Eight
JUAN CARLOS AND THE JEWS

Volumes could be written about King Juan Carlos, his history and his exploits from the time that he faced-down the rebellion of the Generals.

> Feb. 25, 1981, The Arizona Republic: With the surrender of civil guards who seized the Congress of Deputies and held 350 members hostage for 18 hours, Spanish democracy has withstood its severest test yet.
>
> *The hero is 43-year-old King Juan Carlos I, probably the most remarkable leader of any nation in the world today...*

— to his selfless display of courage and ability when he "dived into the sea fully clothed to rescue two sisters whose small boat had capsized off the coast of the island of Majorca. He helped the women aboard his launch and then towed their boat back to harbor," according to a *Reuters* dispatch in The Chicago Tribune July 30, 1990.

Juan Carlos began his reign immediately after the death of Gen. Francisco Franco, having his coronation and grand reception on Nov. 27, 1975. He has been honored by countries and universities worldwide and also was the first European monarch to receive the coveted Charlemagne Prize presented to outstanding leaders "for deserving services in the defense of European ideals."

In 1983, at UNESCO headquarters in Paris, King Juan Carlos and Queen Sofia received "a warm reception by the delegates of 161 countries" and heard the director-general of the organization, M Bow, declare: "This is not a courtesy but the acknowledgement by the international community of the work they have done to foster democracy."

On *June 8, 1984,* from Cambridge, Mass., Assoc. Press reported: "King Juan Carlos of Spain, who attended Harvard... was awarded an honorary doctor of laws degree by the school at its 333rd commencement.

"Juan Carlos, 46, delivered the commencement address Thursday to 25,000 graduates, alumni and family members at the ceremony."

Feb., 1985, SPAIN: The king, don Juan Carlos, has received an honorary degree from the Complutense University of Madrid. This is the first time the Spanish University has distinguished the King with this award, *already received by him from various European and American universities.*

THE KING AND QUEEN AND THE JEWS

From the very beginning of their reign, King Juan Carlos I and Queen Sofia have reached out to the Jewish community of the world. Just four months after the coronation, Queen Sofia made the first move:

> *Mar. 29, 1976, Los Angeles Times:* MADRID - Queen Sophia of Spain attended Sabbath services at Madrid's only synagogue Friday night. The 37-year-old queen may have been the first member of a royal Roman Catholic family to attend services in a synagogue in Spanish history.
>
> The Beth Jacob Synagogue made special arrangements for the queen. It is an Orthodox congregation. The services were in the rites of the Sephardic branch of the Jewish religion, the branch that descended from the original Jews of Spain.

Soon after, King Juan Carlos met with American Jewish leaders.

June 4, 1976, (AP) L.A. Times: WASHINGTON - Departing from a policy observed by Spanish heads of state for the last five centuries, Spain's King Juan Carlos I met Thursday with a delegation of American Jewish leaders. Former Supreme Court Justice Arthur Goldberg, who headed the 11-member delegation said it was the first meeting between a Spanish head of state and a Jewish delegation of any nationality since before 1492, when Jews were expelled from Spain.

Oct. 4, 1987, Jerusalem Post: LOS ANGELES - Six shofars sounded in unison last week as Their Majesties, King Juan Carlos I and Queen Sofia of Spain walked into the packed sanctuary at Sephardic Temple Tifereth Israel, becoming, it is believed, the first Spanish monarchs to enter a synagogue. The 40-minute ceremony was conducted in Ladino, the Judeo-Spanish dialect preserved by Sephardim.

In his welcoming words, Rabbi Jacob Ott spoke of the golden age of Spanish Jews and their signal part in Christopher Columbus's voyage of discovery. However, he also reminded the king of the Inquisition.

Juan Carlos, responding in Spanish, praised the contributions of Sephardim throughout the ages, but did not avoid the darker pages in his country's history.

"I would like to convey to this community the greetings of a Spain which in full conscience assumes the responsibility for the negative as well as the positive aspects of its historic past," he said.

As a thick wedge of security men ushered the royal couple out of the sanctuary, Rabbi Ott reported that the king turned to him in farewell and said that "this experience has been the highlight of my American trip."

DIPLOMATIC RELATIONS

It was on January 17, 1986 that Spain and Israel signed the accord that established full diplomatic relations between the two countries.

KING JUAN CARLOS INVITED TO ISRAEL

June 27, 1991, Jerusalem Post: MADRID - Before meeting here yesterday with Spanish Premier Felipe Gonzalez, Foreign Minister David Levy met with King Juan Carlos in Granada.

During their meeting, Levy delivered a message from President Herzog, inviting the king to visit Israel. The king accepted and said that March 31, 1992 would be a highly symbolic date to be in Jerusalem, as it is the 500th anniversary of the signing of the decree expelling the Jews from Spain.

When March 31, 1992 came around, however, King Juan Carlos said that he could not come to Israel due to the grave illness of his father, Don Carlos. Instead, the following event of significance took place in Madrid.

April 1, 1992, Special to The New York Times, MADRID, March 31, 1992 -In a poignant ceremony marking the 500th anniversary of the expulsion of the Jews from Spain, President Chaim Herzog of Israel and King Juan Carlos of Spain prayed together in the synagogue of Madrid today in a gesture symbolizing reconciliation between their people.

For Mr. Herzog, it was an occasion that "closes one more of the many painful cycles in the history of our people." And he added: "We cannot change the past, But we can learn its lessons and thus assure a better future for ourselves and humanity."

For Juan Carlos, it was a chance both to pay homage to the exiled Sephardic Jewish communities that had never forgotten their Spanish roots and to tell Jews that Sefarad - the Hebrew name for Spain - was "no longer nostalgia" because the country was once again their home.

The King, who wore a skullcap, was accompanied here by Queen Sofia. "It may seem odd to choose the anniversary of a separation for a meeting of such profound significance," he said. "But the history of *all* people and, without doubt, that of Spain, is full of lights and shadows."

START OF THE JERUSALEM COVENANT

On the same day that King Juan Carlos of Spain and President Chaim Herzog of Israel prayed together in the synagogue in Madrid, Jerusalem Day, May 31, 1992, the now-established JERUSALEM COVENANT was launched on its yearlong journey around the world to gain the approval of and the ultimate signatures of outstanding Jewish leaders. Was this a coincidence or was it a divinely-instituted procession of events leading up to "the time of the end"?

King Juan Carlos did not go to Jerusalem as originally planned, due to the illness of his father; but he undoubtedly will do so at a later God ordained date. Since the Jerusalem Covenant was returned to Jerusalem and was presented to President Ezer Weizman for his signature - and for the signatures of "many" other dignitaries on Jerusalem Day, May 19, 1993, can the signature of Juan Carlos, the officially and internationally acclaimed "King of Jerusalem, DEFENDER of Catholic Holy Land interests" be far behind?

MY SUGGESTION

I have a confession to make, and I trust that it was by the inspiration and direction of God's Holy Spirit, for on May 7,

1993 - just 12 days before Jerusalem Day of 1993, I sent by airmail an autographed copy of my book *World War III - When the Arabs Attack Jerusalem* to Ezer Weizman, stating:

> Dear Mr. Weizman: Shalom!
>
> Being aware of the Jerusalem Covenant and the biblical significance of it, I was deeply impressed by the Spirit of G-d to write to you, sending a copy of my most recent Bible-prophecy-related book "WHEN THE ARABS ATTACK JERUSALEM." It has much documented information that is relevant to the world situation, and especially to that which concerns Israel.
>
> I am sure that you are aware of the prophecies of Ezekiel concerning the coming attack, but my many years of research and deep Bible study may (and I trust, will) add to your knowledge.
>
> Pertaining to the Jerusalem covenant, which states: "We love you, O Jerusalem... Forevermore, our home shall be with you," it is self-evident that it will arouse much Islamic indignation. Its affixed signatures of "many" dignitaries from around the world will add to their displeasure.
>
> As a climaxing declaration of this final Covenant, if you already have not done so: may I suggest that a "seal" of this great Jerusalem covenant could be accomplished by inviting King Juan Carlos I of Spain to come to Jerusalem during the High Holy Days of 1993 so that he, as the holder of the official title, "King of Jerusalem, defender of Catholic Holy Land interests" could publicly sign and CONFIRM this Magna Carta of the State of Israel.
>
> It also would fulfill the prophecy of Daniel 9 : 27, regardless of his later actions.
>
> Most sincerely presented, DR. CHARLES R. TAYLOR, President Today In Bible Prophecy, Inc.

My Christian friends, can you grasp the significance of the timing of this suggestion? The Covenant of Daniel 9:27 already, in spite of our unawareness of it until recently, is an eternally planned and executed entity. It exists today as a positive proof of the authenticity, the accuracy and the advance foreknowledge and predestination of Almighty God. Only by the inspiration of and the direction of the Holy Spirit of God could the prophet Daniel write almost 2,500 years ago that such a covenant would be prepared and would be signed by so "many" of the returned children of Israel,[1] ready to be CONFIRMED by "the prince who shall come," the one who is soon to become "the king"[2] of the end time.[3]

If President Weizman is so inclined and he feels led of the Lord to extend the invitation to the King as suggested; and if King Juan Carlos responds by coming to the Holy City of Jerusalem to officially sign the JERUSALEM COVENANT by or on Feast of Tabernacles at the close of the High Holy Days this September, it will be 14 days AFTER the Feast of Trumpets, Rosh Hashana, the first day of the fiscal calendar of the Jewish year AND THE MOST LIKELY DAY FOR THE RAPTURE OF THE CHURCH-IF THIS IS THE YEAR OF OUR LORD'S COMING down to cloud level to receive His Body, the Church, unto Himself, THAT WHERE HE IS, THERE WE MAY BE ALSO.

In Bible terminology in relation to the 70 weeks of Daniel, that would be the equivalent of the "one hour" of Rev. 17:13: for if one week is seven years, then one day is one year and one hour is $1/24$th of a 12-month year, or one-half of a month = two weeks of time. That span of time would give the European Community two weeks to rule "with" the one referred to as the beast in Rev. 17 and to "have one mind and give their power and strength

1. Ezek. 37:16-25   2. Dan. 11:36   3. Dan. 11:40

(authority) unto the beast," the endtime king: so that he could sign the prophesied and prepared JERUSALEM COVENANT with their full backing and authority.

Is this the year? Only our Lord God knows for sure, but everything seems to be lined up and ready for it - in God's perfect time.

Furthermore, there is no other person in all of Europe or the Middle East that has anywhere near the Bible-prophesied qualifications to possibly become THE ANTICHRIST. No one else has the status, the international travel and acceptance, the rapport with the Jewish community and the nation of Israel, the royal background, the Catholic background and the close affinity with the Pope of Rome. Indeed, I say to you, "WATCH KING JUAN CARLOS!"

Please Let ME Be King of Revived Rome!

King Juan Carlos with Pope Paul VI — 1977

King Juan Carlos with Pope John Paul II — 1988

Chapter Nine

WHAT WILL HAPPEN NEXT?

Preliminary events that are prophesied in the Bible relative to the approaching of the seven-year "time of the end" of Dan. 11:40, of the "time of Jacob's trouble" of Jer. 30:7 and of "the times of the Gentiles" of Luke 21:24 and Romans 11:25 commonly called the Tribulation Period, have been coming to pass throughout this generation and now are almost complete. Not only are the nations in their prophesied alignment, either *for* or *against* the nation of Israel, but the Church Age rapidly is falling into the last category thereof as stated in Rev. 3:14-22. Much of the formal church is compromising and is weak, as prophesied, and is "Lukewarm" in its function. Those in the social-gospel-churches are more concerned about their own well-being or for the physical and sociological help of others than about the spiritual salvation of those who are lost.

We do praise God, however, for the faithful endeavors of the true church, the Body of Christ, and for the millions who now are being brought to Christ by the mass-media communications of radio, television, videos and the printed page; and for the dedicated servants of our Lord who do the work. When the last soul has been reached in this Church Age, *then* Jesus will come "with a shout, the voice of the arch angel and the trump of God, and we shall (all) be caught up in the clouds to meet the Lord in the air." What a Day of rejoicing that will be! Following that will be "the time of the end."

MODERN TECHNOLOGY

Today, modern technology is producing the elements needed for the fulfillment of many events "at the time of the end." Only in this generation do we have *television* whereby "all the world" can see the two witnesses of Rev. 11:7-12 when they will be slain in Jerusalem at the middle of the Tribulation. Only in this century do we see the fulfillment of Nahum 2:4

> The chariots shall rage in the streets, they shall jostle one another in the broad ways: they shall seem like torches, they shall run like the lightnings.

And only since 1945 has there been nuclear fission producing heat far greater than the sun whereby one-third of the land area of the earth shall be burned up and one-third of the ships of the seas destroyed by fire as prophesied for the world right AFTER the Rapture of the Church, when the Arabs and their eastern European partners attack Jerusalem and are so mightily opposed by Western Europe and the United States of America, as portrayed in Rev. 8:7-12, which describes the event.

> The first angel sounded, and there followed hail and fire mingled with blood, and they were cast upon the earth: and the third part of trees was burnt up, and all green grass was burnt up.
>
> And the second angel sounded, and as it were a great mountain burning with fire was cast into the sea: and the third part of the sea became blood:
>
> And the third part of the creatures that were in the sea, and had life, died; and the third part of the ships were destroyed.
>
> And the third angel sounded, and there fell a great star from heaven burning as it were a lamp, and it fell upon the third part of the rivers, and upon the fountains of waters;

And the name of the star is called Wormwood: and the third part of the waters became wormwood; and many men died of the waters, because they were made bitter, poisonous.

And the fourth angel sounded, and the third part of the sun was smitten, and the third part of the moon, and the third part of the stars: so that the third part of them was darkened, and the day shone not for a third part of it, and the night likewise.

This, my friends, is truly a graphic description of exactly the known scientific results that will be evident in any nuclear war.

God prophesied as to the magnitude of this great thermonuclear war through His prophet, Isaiah, who wrote in Isa. 13:4-8,

The noise of a multitude in the mountains, like as a great people; a tumultuous noise of the KINGDOMS OF NATIONS GATHERED TOGETHER: THE LORD OF HOSTS MUSTERETH THE HOST OF THE BATTLE.

They come from a far country, from the ends of heaven (and the USA is on the opposite side of the globe from Russia and the Middle East), even the Lord, and THE WEAPONS OF HIS INDIGNATION, TO DESTROY THE WHOLE LAND.

Howl ye, for the day of the Lord is at hand; it shall come AS a destruction from the Almighty...They shall be amazed one at another: THEIR FACES SHALL BE AS FLAMES.

In Isa. 24:5 and 6, he elaborates, "The earth also is defiled under the inhabitants thereof, because they have transgressed the laws, changed the ordinances, broken the everlasting covenant...Therefore the inhabitants of the earth ARE BURNED, AND FEW MEN LEFT." Such will be the results of the soon-coming war at the very beginning of the 7-year Tribulation Period.

Only in this computer age could mankind have the capacity to control buying and selling on a worldwide scale. In Amman, Jordan, while on a tour to Petra in 1974, I went into a local grocery store and found items already over there with UPC code markings, and that was almost 20 years ago. Now, the great international computer in Brussels, Belgium has the capacity to give an identifying number to and keep the records on every man, woman and child on the face of the earth. It did have to be developed, however, and now it exists, making it possible for '"the mark of the beast" to be administered whenever the appropriate time comes. It is no danger to you nor to any of us today, for it is just a convenient computer number, but when the Devil, Satan, Lucifer is cast out of his position in the skies at the middle of the tribulation era and is then confined to the earth as prophesied in Rev. 12:7-12, he will have his endtime king slain and will enter into that king's body in order to receive the worship of mankind which he always wanted, having said in Isa. 14:14, "I WILL BE LIKE THE MOST HIGH."

Declaring himself as the king of this world, Satan within this king will commission his high priest to make an image that can speak and to put that image of him in the by then rebuilt Jewish Temple in Jerusalem, even as it is recorded in Rev. 13, verses 15-18, quote,

> And he had power to give life unto the image of the beast (king), that the image of the beast should both speak, and cause that as many as would not worship the image of the beast should be killed.
>
> And he causeth all, both small and great, rich and poor, free and bond, TO RECEIVE A MARK IN THEIR RIGHT HAND, OR IN THEIR FOREHEAD:

And that no man might buy or sell, save he that had
the mark or the name of the beast, or the number of
his name.

Here is wisdom. Let him that has understanding
count the number of the beast: for it is the number of a
man; and his number is 666.

This is a very remarkable prophecy in that the Lord God by
His Holy Spirit led the Apostle John to write this prophecy
and this specific number of the end time beast-king and of
his international computer code number in A.D. 90 - 1900
years ago, and then caused intelligent men to devise the
computer system in such a manner that 666 is the most
useable number in the world and that it should become the
international code number for the control computer at the
headquarters of the Common Market, the commercial
conglomerate of world trade and communication!

THE ULTIMATE CONGLOMERATE

Satan's greatest effort to take over this world will be made
manifest just as soon as the Rapture of the Church takes
place when the hindering factor of the true believing Church
is removed from Planet Earth "in a moment, in the twinkling of an eye," as prophesied in 1 Corin. 15:52.

Satan's liars and false doctrines have been in the world
ever since Cain killed his brother Abel and was sent away
from Adam and Eve. His descendants became so wicked that
God had to destroy them with the great flood in the days of
Noah. But Noah, a descendant of Seth, a brother of Cain and
Abel "found grace in the eyes of the Lord" and was spared in
the ark.

God established Noah and his family, confirming an everlasting covenant with them in the sign of the rainbow in the
clouds. One of his sons was Shem, a very righteous man, and
of his descendants came Eber, "the Hebrew" who also was

the forefather of Abram, whose name God changed to Abraham.

GOD'S COVENANT

In Genesis 17:1-8, we read:

> And when Abram was ninety years old and nine, the Lord appeared to Abram, and said unto him, "I am Almighty God: walk before me, and be thou perfect, and I will make my covenant between me and thee, and will multiply thee exceedingly.
>
> And Abram fell on his face: and God talked with him, saying, As for me, behold, my covenant is with thee, and thou shalt be a father of many nations. Neither shall thy name any more be called Abram, but thy name shall be ABRAHAM, for a father of many nations have I made thee.
>
> And I will make thee exceeding fruitful, and I will make nations of thee, and kings shall come out of thee. And I will establish my covenant between me and thee and thy seed after thee in their generations for an everlasting covenant, to be a God unto thee, and to thy seed after thee. And I will give unto thee, and to thy seed after thee, the land wherein thou art a stranger, ALL THE LAND OF CANAAN, FOR AN EVERLASTING POSSESSION; and I will be their God."

God renewed that covenant with Abraham's son Isaac and with Isaac's son Jacob, whose name also God changed to Israel, which means "A prince of God."

Again at Bethel, God appeared to Jacob, as recorded in Gen. 35:10-12:

> And God said unto him, "Thy name is Jacob: thy name shall not be called anymore Jacob, but ISRAEL shall be thy name: and he called his name Israel (which means, "A prince of God").

And God said unto him, I am God Almighty: be fruitful and multiply; a nation and a company of nations shall be of thee, and kings shall come out of thy loins; and THE LAND, WHICH I GAVE ABRAHAM AND ISAAC, TO THEE I WILL GIVE IT, AND TO THY SEED AFTER THEE WILL I GIVE THE LAND."

DAVID TAKES JERUSALEM

Five hundred years later, when the children of Israel had come out of the land of Egypt and had conquered most of the land of Canaan, David became king. He ruled first in Hebron, but then he attacked and conquered the Jebusite city of Jerusalem and moved there, calling it the city of David. From that day forward, Jerusalem has been the center of world history.

God verified His covenant again, saying in Psalm 89:34-37,

MY COVENANT WILL I NOT BREAK, nor alter the thing that is gone out of my lips. Once again have I sworn by my holiness, that I will not lie unto David. His seed shall endure for ever, and his throne as the sun before me. It shall be established for ever as the moon, and as a faithful witness in heaven.

Once more, at the dedication of Solomon's Temple on Mt. Moriah in Jerusalem, the Lord declared in 2 Chronicles 6:6,

I HAVE CHOSEN JERUSALEM, THAT MY NAME MIGHT BE THERE; AND HAVE CHOSEN DAVID TO BE OVER MY PEOPLE ISRAEL.

From the lineage of David, Jesus was born where David was born - in the city of Bethlehem. And when Satan's "time of the end" has come to its close, Jesus will defeat him at Jerusalem as recorded in Zechariah 14!

BACKGROUND PREPARATIONS
FOR THE CONFLICT

1948 was THE YEAR OF BEGINNINGS.

In 1948, ISRAEL became a nation again after 2,500 years of exile.

In 1948, the WORLD COUNCIL OF CHURCHES had its first meeting in Amsterdam. In itself, it is not the great harlot church of Revelation 17, seen coming on the world scene as a woman of adultery riding on the back of the seven-headed beast that had ten horns, representing the seven Gentile nations to rule over Jerusalem in "the times of the Gentiles" and having ten horns, representing the final 10-nation entity of the Revived Roman Empire. But it does represent the beginning of that worldwide church entity of falseness that shall prevail during the Tribulation Period. That New Age composite will grow out of the statement of WCC leader Eugene Carson Blake who said: *"The WCC radically challenges each separate church and each section to lose itself into a single worldwide communion."*

In 1948, Luxembourg, The Netherlands and Belgium signed the Benelux Agreement that became the foundation stone for the European Common Market which came into its fullness as the start of the final Roman entity. In 1957, Italy, France, West Germany, Luxembourg, Belgium and The Netherlands signed the TREATY OF ROME. Britain Denmark and Ireland joined in 1973, and Greece became the tenth member Jan. 1, 1981, with Spain and Portugal becoming numbers 11 and 12 on Jan. 1, 1986. Austria has been invited in and has applied for full membership, which will make the ultimate 13, from which the Bible states in Dan. 7:8 and 24 that the end time (Tribulation) king will, quote, "uproot" three of the first kings, meaning of the first ten, bringing the 13 nation entity back to the final revised and revived Roman Empire. Since this is to be done by the king of the Tribulation Period, How very near we must be to the time of the Rapture of the Church, which must take place before he can come into his final authority, uproot the three that are not members of the Western European Union which is the military arm of the European Community, being Denmark, Greece and Ireland: so that the remaining ten can fulfill the prophecy of Rev. 17:12 and 13 which reads,

> And the ten horns which thou sawest are ten kings, which have received no kingdom as yet (not in the days of John who wrote the Revelation in A.D. 90); but receive power as kings one hour with the beast.
>
> These have one mind, and shall give their power and strength (and authority) unto the beast, (referring to the king of the end time)...

Accordingly, we have three entities coming into existence for action in these last days, all having started in "the year of beginnings," 1948; and there is one more.

In 1948, when he was just ten years of age, Prince Juan Carlos of Spain was sent to Madrid to begin his training to become the next king of Spain. Under the direction of Generalissimo Francisco Franco, the military Dictator of Spain, Juan Carlos received his vast strategic academic and military training already documented for you in this presentation. Today, he is the most highly trained and capable military man in the world, is the most travelled and most honored monarch in the world, is a citizen of both Rome and of Madrid and carries the honorary title, *"King of Jerusalem, defender of Catholic Holy Land interests."* All of the documentations of this presentation are vital evidences that this person, King Juan Carlos I of Spain, may be destined to soon become THE KING of the end time, the one commonly referred to as THE ANTICHRIST.

That which he will do, however, has been greatly misunderstood.

NO PEACE AGREEMENT!

THERE HAS BEEN A GREAT MISCONCEPTION about the order of events that are to occur right after the Rapture of the Church.

Not knowing of or even anticipating such a factor as the JERUSALEM COVENANT, which proclaims and declares that Jerusalem is and for ever shall be the Jewish capital of the State of Israel, most of the Bible prophecy preachers and teachers have followed a very false concept that there is to be a "peace agreement" either with or negotiated by "the king" of the end time that will (THEY ERRONEOUSLY SAY) give Israel three and a half years of peace. This concept is totally false! There is *no* mention of any peace agreement in Dan. 9:27 or any place else in the Scriptures.

Their idea comes from an erroneous interpretation of Dan. 8:25, which states, quote:

> And through his policy also he shall cause craft to prosper in his hand; and he shall magnify himself in his heart, and by peace shall destroy (Hebrew - *shachath;* ruin, corrupt, destroy) many: he shall also stand up against the Prince of princes: but he shall be broken without hand.

They are correct in applying this statement to the antichrist king, for that is verified by the statement that (at the end of the tribulation era) "he shall stand up against the Prince of princes" (meaning by then the King of kings - our Lord Jesus when He comes in power and glory as recorded in Rev. 19:21). That the king shall be "broken without hand" is verified by 2 Thess. 2:8 which states, "whom the Lord shall consume with the spirit of his mouth, and destroy with the brightness of his coming." His destiny is defined in Rev. 19:20 which says, "And the beast was taken, and with him the false prophet... These both were cast alive into a lake of fire burning with brimstone."

During the *first half* of the Tribulation Period, however, this end time king is to be Satan's counterfeit ruler on earth while Satan continues to dominate the world from his position of "prince of the power of the air." Satan does not enter the slain body of the antichrist king until the middle of the Tribulation Period when that old Devil is thrown out of the heavens by Michael and his angels as recorded in Rev. 12:7-12, verse 9 stating:

> And the great dragon was cast out, that old serpent, called the Devil and Satan, which deceiveth the whole world: he was cast out into the earth, and his angels (demons) were cast out with him.

IT IS IMPORTANT to realize this Bible prophecy fact, for the king's actions during the first half are by the authority of the Devil, whereas during the last half of the Tribulation Period, the Devil is IN him.

This king has to be in the world today, for all signs point to the near return of our Lord for His Body, the Church, for it (that is, "we") *shall* be taken out of Satan's king's way, and *then he can begin* his endtime function. This is borne out by 2 Thess. 2:7-10 which states:

> For the mystery of iniquity (the plan of Satan) doth already work (already is evident): only he (the Bible-believing Body of Christ of which he is the head, per Col. 1:18) will hinder (hold back the king's real ambitions), until he (that is, we Christians) be taken out of the way... And THEN shall the Wicked One be revealed (presented to all of the remaining ones of the earth): even him whose coming is after the working of Satan with all power and signs and lying wonders, and with all deceivableness of unrighteousness in them that perish: because they received *not* the love of the truth

(did not believe and accept the Gospel of salvation by faith in Jesus), that they might be saved.

It is not the Christians that are to be deceived, but it is to be the unbelievers who refused the knowledge of and the preaching of the truth. Not being saved and not being in the Rapture of the Church, most of them will believe the New Age concepts and the lies of the antichrist king and thusly fulfil the prophecy of 2 Thess. 2:12

> That they all might be damned who believed not the truth, but had pleasure in unrighteousness.

They preferred their sins, and will fall prey to the Devil's lies. Now their only possibility to get to be with us in heaven and with the Lord will be to defy the One World system and its false church of worldwide unity and to die as martyrs for the cause of Christ. Great numbers will, for Rev. 6:9-11 tells of their being slain and then seen in heaven:

> And when he had opened the fifth seal (of the end time judgments of the Tribulation Period), I saw under the altar (in heaven) the souls of them that were slain for the word of God, and for the testimony which they held: And they cried with a loud voice, saying, "How long, O Lord, holy and true, dost thou not judge and avenge our blood on them that dwell on the earth? And white robes were given unto every one of them; and it was said unto them, that they should rest yet for a little season until their fellow servants and also their brethren should be slain as they were, should be fulfilled."

Chapter Ten

VITAL CHRONOLOGY

When the Rapture of the Church takes place and the Jewish "time of Jacob's trouble" starts to unfold, the very first event, at the opening of the first seal of end time judgments, the Devil will give great "power and signs and lying wonders" to his antichrist king. He will step forward on the world scene with "all deceivableness of unrighteousness" evidently utilizing some of his black cult Satanic powers and will so impress the leaders of the Common Market, European Community, that they will make him the leader of all of Western Europe. Austria immediately will join with them for its own protection from the anarchies and communists still prevailing in the Eastern European region, and the EC will have its 13th member. Then, as prophesied in Dan. 7:8 and 24, this King will subdue, eliminate,three of the first ten of the nations to join the Economic Community, namely Denmark, Ireland and Greece, for only these three are not members of the Western European Union, which is the military arm of the E.C. For self protection and also to be able to work in united fashion to protect Israel from the onslaught of the Soviets and Arabs, the three non-members will be "uprooted" by the king, for it is so declared that "HE SHALL SUBDUE THREE OF THE FIRST."

By then, the Arabs and their Soviet and Eastern European anti-Semitic allies will be so threatening that the prophecy of

Rev. 17:12 and 13 shall come to its fulfillment when the EC & Western European Union shall, quote,

> Have one mind, and shall give their power and strength (their authority) unto the beast.

With the backing and approval and authority of all of Western Europe, THE KING, King Juan Carlos as head of the Revived Roman Empire, can then - with much ceremony and as "King of Jerusalem, defender of Catholic Holy Land interests" - go to Jerusalem and sign the already prepared JERUSALEM COVENANT, and thusly "CONFIRM THE COVENANT WITH MANY" Israeli dignitaries and therefore be fully committed to the protection of the nation of Israel.

Daniel 9:27 will be fulfilled, and that of Rev. 6:2 be ready to be activated and the Tribulation Period will be under way.

PEACEFUL DELAY

There will be a peaceful delay, for this is specifically prophesied in the Bible, but it will not be any 3½ years as so many seem to teach. More likely, the time span will be about two weeks while the E.C. makes its changes and the Muslims and Soviets make final preparations for the military attack against the land of Israel, realizing that the USA and Western European powers are in at least temporary disarray due to the sudden disappearance of millions of Bible-believing Christians in the Rapture.

Revelation 7 declares the biblical reason for the delay, however, for it is a direct order of an angel of God:

> And after these things (of Rev. 2 and 3 which outlined the events of the Church Age), I saw four angels...holding the four winds of the earth, that the wind should not blow on the earth, nor on the sea, nor on any tree. And I saw another angel ascending from the east, having the seal of the living God: and he cried

with a loud voice to the four angels, to whom it was given to hurt the earth and the sea, saying, Hurt not the earth, neither the sea, nor the trees, till we have sealed the servants of our God in their foreheads.

And I heard the number of them that were sealed: and there were sealed an hundred and forty and four thousand of all the tribes of the children of Israel.

These 144,000 servants of the living God are sealed for two purposes. One is for their protection from harm during the time of their mission; and the other is for the anointing of the seal of God upon them as they go forth as God's servants to preach THE GOSPEL OF THE KINGDOM as prophesied by Jesus that it should be preached to all the world before He returns at His Second Coming as the King of kings and Lord of lords as revealed in Revelation 19.

No harm is to come to "the earth or the sea or any tree" on the earth until these 144,000 have been sealed and commissioned. In this interim, also, the two special witnesses from heaven, Enoch and Elijah, both of whom have never suffered physical death, but were taken alive into heaven for God's special reason to prepare them for this end-time ministry, will appear in Jerusalem as prophesied in Rev. 11:3-6. Their ministry will be in the city of Jerusalem, whereas the 144,000 ministers from the 12 tribes of Israel will be preaching THE GOSPEL OF THE KINGDOM all over the earth as evidenced by Rev. 7:9-14, which reads in part,

After this (at the conclusion of their ministry at the middle of the Tribulation Period), I beheld, and, lo, a great multitude, which no man could number, of all nations, and kindreds, and tongues, stood before the throne (in heaven) and before the Lamb (of God: Jesus), clothed with white robes, and palms in their hands: and cried with a loud voice, saying, Salvation to our God which sitteth upon the throne, and unto the Lamb...

> And one of the elders said unto me, What are these which are arrayed in white robes (the white robes of the righteousness of Christ), and whence came they? And I said unto him, Sir, thou knowest. And he said to me, These are *they* which came out of great tribulation, and have washed their robes, and made them white in the blood of the Lamb.

In other words, These are people who believed the gospel of the kingdom and were saved by the grace of God and their sins were washed away by the blood of the Lamb, just as any other believer in Jesus Christ as Redeemer.

God never leaves the world without a witness, a manner of salvation. In the Old Testament times, they had the priests and the sacrifices pointing to the supreme Lamb of God who would shed His blood for their redemption. In the Church Age, there has been the ministers and missionaries, teaching and preaching the gospel of the grace of God, "For by grace are ye saved through faith; and that not of yourselves: it is the gift of God: lest any man should boast"; next, the gospel of the kingdom will be preached on the earth after the Rapture of the Church and while they can, being sealed for their protection from Satan and his false church henchmen,until their work is finished at the middle of the Tribulation Period.

Whereas it is written that Jesus said, "I will build my church, and the gates of hell shall not prevail against it," Satan cannot today kill all of the ministers and missionaries, although he tries hard enough. But at the middle of the Tribulation, when the work of the 144,000 is finished as well as the work of the two special witnesses in Jerusalem, it is prophesied in Rev. 11:7 that When they shall have finished their testimony, the beast that ascendeth out of the bottomless pit (Satan, himself, for he is the only one to be released from that pit as recorded in Rev. 20:7) shall make war against them, and shall overcome them, and kill them. This is a

strong evidence that the Church is not in any portion of the
Tribulation Period, for Satan cannot prevail against the total
Church, but he does overcome and kill the 144,000
witnesses, for they are seen in Rev. 14 as being in heaven
with the Lamb of God, being, quote, "redeemed from the
earth." The two special witnesses will be seen to ascend
bodily up to heaven after their being slain in Jerusalem when
their work is finished.

Then the Lord provides another witness which cannot be
slain, for it is an angel flying through the skies proclaiming
THE EVERLASTING GOSPEL during the last half of the
Tribulation Period while Satan is limited to the earth because
he was thrown out of the skies by Michael the arch angel in
Rev. 12. This angelic minister will preach to all the world for
the last half of the Tribulation, until the last martyr has been
slain and the Bride of Christ is complete, for the martyrs of
the entire Tribulation Period will be joined with the raptured
Church, which is THE BODY OF CHRIST, to constitute the
redeemed of *all* of the ages, becoming the Bride of Christ,
called to the great and wonderful Marriage Supper of the
Lamb as recorded in Rev. 19:7-9,

> Let us be glad and rejoice, and give honor to him:
> for the marriage of the Lamb is come, and his wife hath
> made herself ready.
>
> And to her was granted that she should be arrayed in
> fine linen, clean and white: for the fine linen is the
> righteousness of saints.
>
> And he said unto me, Write, Blessed are they which
> are called to the marriage supper of the Lamb.

This has been a brief summary of the spiritual factors and
the ministers of the gospel during the Tribulation Period,
from the Rapture to the Marriage Supper with all of the
saints of all the ages just before Jesus comes back to the earth
in His Second Coming as the King of kings and Lord of lords

to destroy the works of the devil and to eliminate all of his armies at the great Battle of Armageddon so that Jesus can establish His perfect rule on earth for the 1,000 years of the millennium, at last bringing Peace on Earth.

EVENTS AFTER THE SEALING
OF THE 144,000

While the 144,000 Jewish witnesses are being sealed for service and for their protection, and while their enemies, the Muslims, are mustering their armies for the "final" assault against Israel, the king of Western Europe's revised and revived Roman empire will be solidifying his position, be exercising supernatural "signs and wonders," and be receiving his power and authority from those who are to be ruling "with him" in the closing days.

Dan. 9:27 specifically declares that he is to "CONFIRM THE COVENANT WITH MANY" Israelis for one week (one week of years - 7 years).

That Jerusalem Covenant already has been prepared, been signed by many Israeli officials and sent around the world and returned to Jerusalem. Now it is ready for his signature. When he does sign it as prophesied, doing so with the full authority of the Western European powers, another Bible prophecy will come into action. Dan. 11:40 proclaims that

> At the time of the end (when the tribulation action
> is set to explode on the world), shall the king of the
> south "push at him."

The Arab League, with its headquarters in the south, being in Cairo, Egypt, is depicted as coming "at *him*" when it attacks Israel. After all, he will be the designated protector of Israel: both by having signed the Jerusalem Covenant declaring that Jerusalem is the eternal capital of the State of Israel "for ever," and also by his being the acknowledged "King of Jerusalem, defender of Catholic Holy Land interests."

King Juan Carlos was born into a Roman Catholic family in the city of Rome, was given Roman Catholic baptism as a babe by Pope Pius XII and has been a devoted Catholic Opus Diesta all of his life.

Yes, the Arabs will "push at him" - will attack him and all of Western Europe and all of the NATO allies thereof, including the U.S.A. And when they do, the 60 million Muslims of the former Soviet Union plus the many anti-Semitic peoples of Eastern Europe of the former Warsaw Pact nations will join their ethnic brothers and will "come against him like a whirlwind," firing their nuclear arsenals at the European Community cities and also at the major cities and strategic targets in the United States of America to keep these nations from coming to the aid of Israel.

The devastating results of this war are recorded in the books of Isaiah, Joel, Ezekiel, Daniel, The Revelation and elsewhere in the Bible. The prophet Joel wrote nearly 2,800 years ago,

> O Lord, to thee will I cry: for THE FIRE hath devoured the pastures of the wilderness, and THE FLAME hath burned all the trees of the field. The beasts of the field cry also unto thee: for the rivers of waters are dried up, and THE FIRE hath devoured the pastures of the wilderness.
>
> Blow the trumpet in Zion, and sound an alarm in my holy mountain: let all the inhabitants of the land tremble: for THE DAY OF THE LORD COMETH, for it is nigh at hand (all ready to begin its course)...
>
> A fire devoureth before them; and behind them a flame burneth: the land is as the garden of Eden before them, and behind them a desolate wilderness: yea, and nothing shall escape them.

When the nuclear bombs fall, nothing shall escape where they hit, and the Soviets and Arabs today still have over

25,000 nuclear warheads, as also do the Western Allies. The dreaded nuclear holocaust will come, for it is specifically prophesied. Read Rev. 8:7-12 for the details of one third of the earth greatly affected. Praise the Lord that it will be AFTER the Rapture of the Church, and God's believers of today will be in heaven.

NUCLEAR WAR

Chapter Eleven

THE LEGACY OF THE KING

Juan Carlos de Borbon was born January 5, 1938 in Rome, Italy.

Juan Carlos the prince was a "prince-in-waiting" for over a quarter of a century, for he could not become king until the 1975 death of his predecessor Generalissimo Francisco Franco.

As a prince of Spain, however, the 27 years of training gave him the most extensive academic and military training of any monarch in history: from Madrid University to Harvard and through all three of Spain's vaunted academies: the Army, the Navy and the great Saragosa Air Force Academy. He can handle the largest tanks, or ships or aircraft from modern helicopters to the F-18 fighter jets. They say, "He is audacious!"

When Western Europe really needs a top military commander, the Commander-in-Chief of the Spanish Forces is trained, ready and waiting. He now waits only for the strategic moment: when the world leaders will be perplexed and in turmoil when the Rapture of the Church instantly removes millions of the stable, born again Christians from the face of the earth.

To tell of all of his destiny throughout the Tribulation Period would require another full documentation of Bible prophecies. The purpose of this presentation was and is to give to you "the preponderance of the evidence" that it may be King Juan Carlos I of Spain who is the prepared one to become the end time king commonly referred to as THE ANTICHRIST. Most certainly he is the right person in the right place at the right time.

HIS MOMENT

When his moment comes, Rev. 13:2 says that the dragon, Satan, will give this king "his power, and his seat, and great authority," also causing the unsaved leaders of the E.C. nations to, quote, "have one mind, and give *their* power and strength unto the beast." This will launch him on his way to the glory that he desires - and to his ultimate destruction.

As head of the revised Roman empire, and very likely one who will be crowned as such by the Pope of Rome, King Juan Carlos then can sign the Jerusalem Covenant as the king, not only of Spain, but as the king of all of Western Europe and, indeed, as "King of Jerusalem, DEFENDER of Catholic Holy Land interests," and thusly fulfill Daniel 9:27, committing himself and all whom he represents to the defense of Jerusalem as the eternal capital of the nation of Israel.

By way of response, in fury and in full accord with their many declarations of "Down with Israel, and Down with the Great Satan (USA)," the Arabs "of the south" will attack Israel, having promise of help from their Muslim and Soviet friends of "the north" who also will enter the conflict "like a whirlwind" as depicted in Dan. 11:40-43, which also states, "and the land of Egypt shall not escape." Isa. 19:16 says "In that day shall Egypt be like unto women: and it shall be afraid." Isa. 17:1 states further, quote, "The burden of Damascus. Behold, Damascus is taken away from being a city, and it shall be a ruinous heap." In all of history, that has not yet happened, but it will happen soon - when the Arabs attack Jerusalem.

Likewise, the prophet Zephaniah, in Zeph. 2:9 and 10 recorded in the Bible, "As I live, saith the Lord of hosts, the God of Israel, Surely Moab shall be as Sodom (which God destroyed by fire in the days of Abraham), (and Moab and Ammon, with the mountains of Edom, constitute the kingdom of Jordan today), and the children of Ammon (will be) as Gomorrah... a perpetual desolation. This shall they have for their pride, because they have reproached and magnified themselves against the people of the Lord of hosts." It is in Jordan that the Palestinians have railed the most against the returned remnant of the children of Israel, the Israelis of today, and God says of it, "The residue of my people shall spoil them, and the remnant of my people shall possess them."[1]

Jordan is the only area in the Middle East that will not come under the jurisdiction of the king of Spain and of Rome, because that area contains the protective mountains of Petra and Bozrah in the southern mountains of Edom, which today is a part of Jordan. *Israel will possess that region*, for this is the specific prophecy of the Word of God. It is there that the Orthodox Jews and remnant of believers will flee from Jerusalem at another time - at the middle of the Tribulation Period - when Satan kills his king of Rome so he can possess his body and go into the rebuilt Jewish Temple and demand worship as God as stated in 2 Thess. 2:4.

To take Jordan first, is the Israeli plan according to military reports, in order to split the Arab forces as well as to fulfill their scriptures as I just stated. Israel's nuclear power can burn both Damascus and Ammon, Jordan, and only in this generation of time could that possibly happen, for there was no nuclear capacity until 1945. *Now it can happen* - and soon will!

The evidence is before us. Israel, the Western European Union leading to the prophesied revived Roman empire, and

1. Zeph. 2:10

the Middle East tensions ready to explode all point to "the time of the end."

YOUR OPTIONS

Not all people will be in the immense war that very soon will be fought over Jerusalem and the land of Israel. Those who have trusted in the Lord and in His shed blood to pay the penalty for their sins and who trust in Him for their salvation will be "caught up" to the glories of heaven before that war takes place.

Will YOU be among them - with us in the Rapture?

The only way to be sure is to get right with God by having your sins forgiven: and we do have the precious promise of God that "Whosoever shall call on the name of the Lord shall be saved." Jesus not only died on a cruel Roman cross to pay the penalty for your sins, but in victory He arose from the dead,-was seen on earth by hundreds of people for 40 days before ascending to heaven, during which time He gave the Great Commission to the church to preach the Gospel to all the world.

I tell you one more time: Believe on the Lord Jesus Christ as your Redeemer and Savior, and you will be saved. Say this "sinner's prayer" with me now in true sincerity:

> Dear Father in heaven: I need your salvation. Like everyone else, I have done wrong and am a sinner. I am sorry for my sins, and right now I ask you to forgive my sins and to save my soul.
>
> I accept the great sacrifice of Jesus when He died on the cross to pay the penalty for the sins of the world, including mine. Thank You, Lord, for buying my pardon with your own blood. Help me to live for you and to be a faithful Christian, telling others of Your great salvation. I now am a child of God by faith in Jesus my Lord. Amen.

Since there is no other option than to live for self indulgence and/or for false New Age doctrines that lead to the worship of Satan, Lucifer, the Devil, your decision determines your destiny: either eternity in God's wonderful heaven or eternity with the Devil in the flames of hell.

Jesus loves you and gave His life for you. Accept His gift of life today!

This salvation message is being proclaimed far and wide as gospel radio, television, the printed page and graphic videos reach out into every country on earth. The outpouring of God's Holy Spirit is drawing millions of people worldwide into the living body of believers in our Lord Jesus Christ.

Conversely, the devil's crowds are flaunting erotic life styles, the gurus of the East are deluding many and false cults are striving to win over the newly freed people of the former Soviet and Communist bloc countries.

The challenge before us today is to help spread the gospel of salvation by grace through faith in our Lord. At Today in Bible Prophecy, I am doing my utmost to make the salvation message a part of every report. In addition to that, God has given me a great commission to also warn the people of our area: primarily all of the U.S. and Canada, that God's severe judgment is about to fall on the ungodly, the pleasure-mad and rebellious ones who are "falling away" from the faith of our fathers.

WE NEED YOUR HELP

You can help in this last round-up of souls and in the sounding of the alarm to the wayward and to the uninformed. Your tax-deductible gift to this ministry of Bible Prophecy for Today will have its reward in heaven.

Please pray with and for us as we document the worldwide news until the very day of His return. Remember also that King Juan Carlos always has befriended the Jewish people, has recognized their nation politically and is committed to their protection. The Antichrist King does not actually become the antiChrist until slain and his body is indwelt by the Devil, Satan, at the middle of the Tribulation Period. That is when the "mark of the beast" will begin.

Today, King Juan Carlos is at peace with Israel and stands firmly in his position as the warrior-guardian of the State of Israel against their sworn enemies, the Islamic people of the Arab and Soviet world. With God's help and with or without divine intervention, those enemies will be defeated and Israel will be free to build its Tribulation Temple in Jerusalem. It all is ready to come to pass.

NO MORE DELAY - NO MORE TIME!?

In this climax of the Ages, as we so rapidly approach the time of the coming of the Lord down to cloud level to "catch up" His Body of believers "That where He is, there we may be also," and the tribulation era begins with the sealing of the 144,000 Jewish witnesses of THE GOSPEL OF THE KINGDOM, which will be the message during "the time of Jacob's trouble," which is the Jewish time period before the coming of their King of kings, the Messiah, we want you to be aware of Satan's deceptions and devices.

Books have been written about the New Age Movement. I can not go into detail concerning it here, but there is a recent development that has been brewing throughout this century, and now is about to explode upon the world.

In Volume 22, No. 1 of *Bible Prophecy News* published the first of this year, I documented the announcement that the World Parliament of Religions is scheduled to have a tremendous meeting in Chicago the last week in August and the first week in September, 1993. Secondary meetings will also be held in Britain, Scotland, Canada, India, Nigeria, Kenya, Australia, Pakistan and New Zealand, but the main conference will be in Chicago. It is there that THE PLAN for the NEW WORLD ORDER of planetary government is to be set and the ONE WORLD RELIGION of global unity established. THE PLAN calls for the Lucifer-honoring One World Religion to be comprised of ALL faiths on Planet Earth, each worshipping its own "higher power" but in worldwide unity.

In the June 1993 issue of *FLASHPOINT,* a publication of Tex Marrs and Living Truth Ministries, he states, "I have been alerting readers of *Flashpoint* to the forthcoming occult assembly in Chicago being called *The Parliament of World Religions.* I reported that Hindu gurus, Buddhist monks, witches, satanic priests, occult leaders, Luciferians, liberal Jewish rabbis, and assorted New Age "dignitaries" would be attending this event. Their joint goal is *UNITY* - to bring all the world's faiths and religions together as one. In other words, these determined men and women are all working furiously to SET UP SATAN'S LAST DAYS WORLDWIDE CHURCH OF THE BEAST, "666." Many of the participants in Chicago are well aware that it is the devil whom they serve. Others are unwitting accomplices to evil, being DECEIVED. In all, occultists and false religionists from over 130 countries will trek to Chicago to celebrate their "UNITY IN DIVERSITY."

Funded mainly with Rockefeller money, the *Parliament of World Religions* will be held in Chicago August 28 - September 4, 1993. IT WILL KICK OFF A *7 YEAR NEW AGE PLAN* first formulated by the *Club of Rome,* a key planning group under the control of the Illuminati hierarchy. THE PLAN CALLS FOR THE INITIATION OF ALL OF HUMANITY BY THE YEAR 2,000, and *that LUCIFER is in charge of our Planetary evolution.*

FOR YOUR INFORMATION

For the latest issue of our quarterly documented news bulletin *Bible Prophecy News* send a contribution of any amount to Bible Prophecy for Today, requesting it by name. That publication also lists our radio log of broadcasts across the USA and Canada, and it lists the many books, cassettes and albums prepared for you by, Dr. Charles R. Taylor. Get these materials and use them to witness to others about the soon coming of our wonderful Lord.

Be a missionary for Jesus by being a supporter of our vital radio broadcast to win and to warn America. Also, you can receive our special Countdown News Letter each month *for the most current information* if you pledge any amount on a regular monthly basis. The Countdown Monthly News Letter is only sent to those who do support by pledging on a regular basis.

May this highly documented presentation be a real blessing to you. Your comments are invited. Please address all orders and correspondence to Bible Prophecy for Today, P.O. Box 5700, Huntington Beach, California 92615-5700. God bless you.

HABSBURG UPDATE ADDENDA
AS OF JULY 1993

The July issue of *VANITY FAIR* carried a major article by Bob Colacello concerning the royal Habsburgs of Europe. Within it we find these details:

(On page 107) ARCHDUKE OTTO von HABSBURG, 80, the son of the last Austro-Hungarian emperor, Charles I, is a member of the European Parliament in Strasbourg. He was to accompany his wife, Archduchess Regina von Habsburg, who was born a royal princess of Germanic Saxony, on their annual pilgrimage to Medugorji, a small town in Bosnia where the Virgin was said to have appeared to a group of children in 1981, but HE HAD TO BE IN MADRID FOR THE FUNERAL OF HIS COUSIN DON JUAN BORBON, father of King Juan Carlos of Spain, who died April 1, 1993.

(On page 131) The hot rumor in Madrid is that (Otto's son) Karl's younger brother, Georg, is to marry Princess Elena, the elder daughter of King Juan Carlos and Queen Sofia.

(On page 132) Having been asked if he thought restoring the monarchy — and there had been some talk of it in the press - would be a good idea, Karl von Habsburg replied: "Frankly, I just don't see it... I think there are more important things to think about and look after, so *I'm* not losing my time for that." He then pointed out that Austria became a republic in 1918 and said, quote, "My name is Karl Habsburg, and that's it. Period." He concluded by stating that he wants to run for office in Austria in the near future, but hasn't committed himself to a political party.

Herein we see Karl's lack of interest in, if not disdain for, any monarchy.

This should put to rest any idea of his becoming the Antichrist!

WATCH KING JUAN CARLOS, AND BE READY FOR THE RAPTURE - VERY SOON!!

Since THE PLAN calls... for all of humanity to take the Luciferian initiation and thereby to worship Lucifer, the Devil, by the year 2,000; and since the Chicago convocation, the *Parliament of World Religions*, is to set forth a *7 YEAR NEW AGE PLAN* by September 4, 1993 to bring this about, is it not highly significant that this meeting concludes just 12 days before Rosh Hashana, the Feast of Trumpets of September 16, 1993? Is this by accident or is it by Divine appointment?

Most assuredly we are at a most critical time in world history and life. BE SURE THAT YOU KNOW THE LORD AND HAVE ASKED JESUS INTO YOUR HEART, that you can be "caught up" with us at the Rapture of the Church, for it could well be that this is the year and the time for that marvellous event. BELIEVE ON THE LORD JESUS CHRIST, AND YOU SHALL BE SAVED. And then live for Him and serve Him with all your heart and soul and life; and help us to alert this sin-cursed nation and world that JESUS IS COMING SOON. Your support is needed now more that at any other time, for our opportunity for soul-winning and for sounding the alarm of soon-coming judgment is almost over.

Let this fully documented presentation be a real challenge to you personally. Read it again slowly and carefully, making a few notes, so you can explain its message to others. Most people have no idea that such a man is so well qualified and prepared to take over a revived Roman empire in Western Europe and as a result of further conquests to control the entire world, already dominating all of Central and South America by his Latin American Conference of Nations, advocating peace and harmony.

In the meantime, in the closing days of this Church Age, you and I have a tremendous challenge to reach all whom we can for salvation: to preach, teach, proclaim and to witness in every manner that we can, warning every one that JESUS IS COMING VERY SOON, and that they need to have their faith in His salvation or else face the tremendous trials and judgments of the seven years of the Tribulation Period. Win them to Jesus so they can be with us in the glorious Rapture of the Church, and greater will be your rewards in heaven.

If you feel limited as to your personal witness, or in addition thereto, help us of BIBLE PROPHECY FOR TODAY to reach the millions of the USA and Canada by radio and the printed page. It is very expensive, but also is very effective in reaching many people who do not go to church. Your gifts to this ministry can result in many, many souls being won to Christ. Let God bless you by blessing your contributions to this vital end time ministry.

EXAMPLES OF CURRENT INFORMATION AVAILABLE

As my research continues, vital information related to Bible prophecy comes to light. These I report in the Countdown Monthly news letter and in Bible Prophecy news. Following are a few samples:

May 3, 1993, Miami Herald: In Russia, nationalists charge that Zionists brought down the Soviet Union and are now tunneling under Russia. In Eastern Europe, they complain that Jews are buying local properties at bargain basement prices. Skinhead gangs from the Baltic to Bucharest share a visceral hatred of Jews, and 100 Polish skinheads shouted "Down with Jews!" as officials marked the anniversary of the Warsaw Ghetto uprising.

Nine of ten Jews living in Moscow, St. Petersburg and Kiev want to leave, according to a poll released in December.

Special Office Brief Intelligence Report

From England, March 16, 1989: "In the supposedly secret Russian discussions between Russia and Islamic countries, Saudi Arabia and Jordan have been guaranteed neutral status if they will on their part not interfere WHEN RUSSIA GIVES THE SIGNAL TO HER PROPOSED ACTIVE PARTNERS TO ATTACK ISRAEL -a conflict calculated (by Russia) to last only three days at the most and therefore one in which the Atlantic Powers cannot possibly intervene. THAT MAY PROVE TO BE ONE OF THE BIGGEST MISCALCULATIONS IN MODERN HISTORY.

UKRAINE'S NUKES

June 23, 1993, Ch. Sci. Monitor: Ukraine became the world's third-largest nuclear power overnight when the Soviet Union broke up. It has the second largest army in Europe.

Ukraine has 1240 nuclear warheads on 130 Russian-made SS-19 missiles and 46 more modern SS-24 missiles made at home, as well as 400 nuclear tipped air-launched cruise missiles.

ELSEWHERE

June 21, 1993, Near East Report: Iran is acquiring ballistic missiles and related production technology from China and North Korea. By the end of 1993, Tehran may initiate production of the North Korean No Dong 1 long-range missile, enabling it to reach the Holy Land 800 miles away. Ten missiles were to have been delivered to Iran in April. Recognition of the potential threat from Iran is essential.

July 19, 1993, Wall St. Journal: There is growing concern about another of Pyongyang's activities: selling ballistic missiles in the volatile Middle East. North Korea is selling to Iran, Libya and Syria its Scud-B

and Scud-C missiles which can carry nuclear devices. It also plans to export its No Dong-I missile, which has the range to reach Israel and even threatens parts of Europe from Libya, say U.S. analysts.

THE REASON

There can be no other purpose for this type of weaponry in the hands of the Islamic nations, but to attack Israel, and if necessary, to attack Israel's Western European defenders!

THE JERUSALEM COVENANT

The Jerusalem Covenant, proclaiming the city of Jerusalem as the capital of the nation of Israel FOR EVER has been produced, gone around the world for a year for verification and approval of top Jewish leaders worldwide and has been signed by "MANY," as prophesied in Dan. 9:27. All it now needs is the signature of THE ANTICHRIST KING - JUAN CARLOS to "CONFIRM" it, and that will happen SOON!

WHY NOT 1993?

The wars, the wickedness, the earthquakes "in many places" the floods, the plagues and the moral decline and killings caused us to greatly hope for and anticipate the coming of our Lord in 1993, but God's perfect time was not quite fulfilled. Looking at the Jewish calendar and reading *The Jerusalem Post,* I discovered:

Sept. 11, 1993, Jerusalem Post: "The Seven-Year Glitch" - Israel is entering the last year of a seven-year sabbatical cycle, a year in which Jews are enjoined by the Torah to let the Land of Israel lie fallow...The Laws of Shmitta seem clear-cut in Lev. 25:2-6, "When ye come into the Land which I give you. then shall the Land keep a Sabbath of rest unto the land...In the seventh year shall be a sabbath unto the Lord: ye shall neither sow your field nor prune your vineyard." This will be the first intifada age shmitta.

COMMENT

The long article describes ways and means of the observance, but to the student of Bible prophecy, another factor looms before us: 1993-94, from Rosh Hashana Sept. 16, 1993 to Sept. 6, 1994, being a year of shmitta, the Jewish sabbatical year for the Lord and the close of the seven-year period, THEN *Rosh Hashana of Sept. 6, 1994 will start the last seven-year cycle of this century,* and most likely will usher in the prophesied seven-year's great Tribulation Period so that the Rosh Hashana (Jewish New Year) of the year 2001 can begin the millennium - the 1,000 year era of the marvellous reign of the Messiah, the Redeemer of both Jew and Gentile!

LET US MAKE THIS YEAR OF GRACE A TIME OF GREAT FERVENCY FOR CHRIST!

THE COUNTDOWN TO THE PEACE ACCORD

Sept. 11, 1993, Los Angeles Times: DAMASCUS, Syria - In a flurry of death threats and angry rhetoric, radical Palestinian groups that represent the most potent guerrilla forces in the Israeli occupied territories rejected on Friday the PLO's peace accord with Israel and vowed to continue their attacks. Jibril, who predicted in an interview that PLO leader Arafat will be assassinated by fellow Palestinians, added: "Time will prove that this is not a peace agreement." Another Palestinian group based in Syria, said in Damascus that it was "Sanctioning the shedding of the blood of this traitor."

Sept. 12, 1993, Jerusalem Post: PLO Chairman Yasser Arafat's security chiefs are taking no chances. His detail has been doubled in recent weeks to as many as 15 heavily armed bodyguards.

Sept. 20, 1993, U.S.News & World Report: The PLO envisions keeping law and order in the West Bank and Gaza with a police force of 20,000 to 30,000 fighters. Hamas is reportedly demanding 30 percent representation in the Palestinian police, reflecting what it says is its political power in the territories. The PLO is likely to reject the demand. Arafat may have a hard time keeping the promises he made last week to quiet the Palestinian intifada. In August alone, Palestinians shot at or threw molotov cocktails at Israeli vehicles 53 times.

COMMENTARY

This closing year of the 7-year cycle is going to be one of "distress among nations, with perplexity," as opposing factions juggle for priority and control. As to Bible prophecy, God declared in Ezek. 37:25, pertaining to Israel, "They shall dwell in the land that I have given Jacob my servant... for ever."

By the interim agreement, Israelis are stalling for time, anxiously hoping for deliverance by the coming of their Messiah. Instead, there will be the Rapture of the Church, then the antichrist king who will defeat the Arabs, and THEN Temple worship followed by desecration until Jesus comes as King of kings!

WHILE AMERICA SLEEPS

July 1993, N.Y. The Defense Department is lifting restrictions on visits to the Pentagon by Russian military officials while oppressive spying by GRU agents continues according to Pentagon officials. "They will now be accredited to enter the Pentagon freely, and with no restraint on their movements. The Russians have not reciprocated."

THE FOX IS IN THE HENHOUSE! Stupid Americans, WAKE UP TO REALITY!

KING JUAN CARLOS HONORED IN ISRAEL

Nov. 20, 1993, Jerusalem Post: King Juan Carlos of Spain and his wife Queen Sofia concluded a historic four-day visit to Israel last week as part of a campaign to normalize relations between Spain and the Jewish people just over 500 years after the Expulsion.

The monarch, who still holds the 13th century title "King of Jerusalem," was received at the Wohl Rose Garden by President Ezer Weizman, and met with a number of political leaders. The king also addressed the Knesset, hosted a delegation of Palestinians at the Spanish consulate in eastern Jerusalem, visited Vad Vashem and the Western Wall, and received an honorary doctorate from the Hebrew University.

"The chemistry was good," was how one official summed up the first state visit by a reigning European monarch. When the royal couple officially took their leave at a ceremony at Beit Hanassi, Weizman called the king "your majesty, my good friend." He thanked the royal couple for "ADDING CONFIDENCE TO THE LEADERS AND PEOPLE OF ISRAEL THAT WE ARE NOT ALONE AS IN PAST YEARS."

At the Church of the Holy Sepulcher. the royal couple genuflected and kissed the tomb and then joined in a Catholic mass. The religious ceremony -clearly the highlight of the visit for the Catholic monarchs - was prolonged, and was followed by a visit to a Spanish convent.

COMMENT

At present, Juan Carlos is the very highly honored King of Spain. However, the Antichrist cannot be revealed to the European public and to the people of the world in the manner in which I have so highly documented his history and destiny in the book and album by that title. It is only AFTER we, the believing Body of Christ, are "caught up" into heaven "in the twinkling of an eye" that 2 Thess. 2:8 will be fulfilled: "And THEN shall that Wicked (One) be revealed with the working of Satan "with all power and signs and lying wonders."

While speaking at the wonderful West Coast Prophecy Conference in Irvine on November 11, 1993, I outlined how his position was in fulfillment of specific Bible prophecies and that the King would, in time, "CONFIRM THE COVENANT WITH MANY" (Israelis), affirming that Jerusalem is and shall be the capital of the state of Israel FOR EVER.

He will, indeed, become THE DEFENDER of Catholic sites in Israel - SOON!

For further current information until Jesus comes for us, send for BIBLE PROPHECY NEWS and the Monthly Countdown Newsletter.

Bible Prophecy For Today

P.O. Box 5700 • Huntington Beach, CA 92615

BOOKS

The Antichrist King — Juan Carlos by Dr. Charles R. Taylor 12.95
Beware America by Dr. Charles R. Taylor 3.95
Chronological Study of the Book of Revelation by Dr. Charles R. Taylor.....................9.95
Death of Sadat — Start of World War III by Dr. Charles R. Taylor 3.95
Parable of the Ten Virgins by Dr. Charles R. Taylor...5.95
Pretribulation Rapture and the Bible by Dr. Charles R. Taylor..................................2.50
Those Who Remain by Dr. Charles R. Taylor 6.95
Saddam's Babylon the Great by Dr. Charles R. Taylor 6.95
When Jesus Comes by Dr. Charles R. Taylor..4.95
World War III — When the Arabs Attack Jerusalem by Dr. Charles R. Taylor..........6.95

CASSETTES

The Antichrist King — Juan Carlos? by Dr. Charles R. Taylor
    (3-cassette album)...16.95
Beware America by Dr. Charles R. Taylor 6.95
Chronological Study of the Book of Revelation by Dr. Charles R. Taylor
    (3-cassette album)...16.95
How to Escape Tribulation Martyrdom by Dr. Charles R. Taylor 6.95
Israel — Key to the Rapture by Rev. Tom Benvenuti...6.95
Life Saving Instructions for Those Who Remain by Dr. Charles R. Taylor 6.95
The Rapture... Pre-, Mid-, or Post-Tribulation? by Rev. Tom Benvenuti 6.95
Rapture Cassette Album by Dr. Charles R. Taylor (3-cassette album) 16.95
    Sound the Alarm!...6.95
    When the Arabs Attack Jerusalem...6.95
    What the Bible Teaches About the Rapture Question 6.95
Rock Music Warning by Dr. Charles R. Taylor 6.95
Saddam's Babylon the Great by Dr. Charles R. Taylor (4-cassette album)................19.95
Sabbath Worship or Sunday Worship by Dr. Charles R. Taylor 6.95
The Seven Churches of Revelation: Then & Now by Rev. Tom Benvenuti
    (3-cassette album)...16.95
When Jesus Comes by Dr. Charles R. Taylor..6.95

OTHER WITNESSING TOOLS AND SPECIAL PUBLICATIONS

The Destiny Chart by Dr. Charles R. Taylor
    (in chronological order, black and white)..2.00
The Destiny Chart by Dr. Charles R. Taylor (18 x 50 multicolor teaching chart) 9.00
666 is Here tract by Dr. Charles R. Taylor (100 tracts)..9.95
Bible Prophecy News (quarterly newsletter)
    1 year subscription for any contribution ...._____
Countdown Monthly Newsletter (pledge of $15 or more per month) ...._____

Shipping and handling to total orders 2.00

Make all checks payable to Bible Prophecy For Today

Name _____Address _____

City _____State _____Zip_____

MOST URGENTLY NEEDED MATERIALS

THE ANTICHRIST KING — JUAN CARLOS is a documentary that is so factual and so biblically correct that it cannot be denied. Born in Rome, a "prince who shall come" for 37 years, receiving the greatest military training of any man in history so that he can go forth "conquering and to conquer" (Rev. 6:3), and a friend of Israel who already has the title "King of Jerusalem, defender of Catholic Holy Land interests." (4-1/2 hour 3-cassette album — $19.95) (Book — $9.95).

WORLD WAR III — WHEN THE ARABS ATTACK JERUSALEM — The Bible pattern of things to come with pictures, maps and documented news showing Bible prophecy fullfillments that proclaim that Jesus IS coming very soon. (Cassette — $8.95) (1992 Edition of the Book — $6.95).

RADIO LOG

KAAY — 1090 AM — Little Rock, AR.............................1:00 pm CT Sat. — All of Arkansas

KAAY — 1090 AM — Little Rock, AR .Midnight Sat. CT — Cen. & Mtn. areas U.S. & Canada

KARI — 550 AM
　　Blaine, WA (Vancouver, BC) ....9:00 pm Sat. — No. Washington and British Columbia

KCKN — 1020 AM — Roswell, NM.......7:30 pm MT Sat. and 9:00 pm Sun. — All MT states

KEXS — 1090 AM — Kansas City, MO..............1:00 pm CT Sunday — Kansas and Missouri

KGER — 1390 AM — Los Angeles & Orange County ....6:30 pm Saturday

KMIL — 1330 AM — Cameron, TX ....6:30 pm Sunday

KRVN — 880 AM — Lexington, NB...11:00 pm CT Friday — All U.S. west of Little Rock, AR

KTWO — 1030 AM — Casper, WY......10:30 pm MT Fri. — All Mtn./Western States, Canada

KXEL — 1540 AM — Waterloo, IA......11:15 pm CT Thursday — Denver to Chicago, Ottowa

WBMD — 750 AM — Baltimore, MD12:30 pm and 7:00 pm ET Sat. — Virginia, New Jersey

WDBA — 107.3 FM — DuBois, PA..8:00 am Sunday

WLVJ — 640 AM
　　Royal Palm Beach, FL ....9:30 pm Sat. and 8:00 am Sunday — S.E. Florida

WRFA — 820 AM — Largo, FL.........................9:15 am ET Sunday — All of Western Florida

WSM — 650 AM — Nashville ....11:30 am CT Saturday and 8:00 pm CT Sunday

WYCA — 92.3 FM
　　Hammond, IN (Chicago)....................10:00 pm CT Thurs. — No. Illinois and No. Indiana

ALL RADIO BROADCASTS are on audio cassette. Single programs are $6.00 each, or get all 4 or 5 broadcasts of the month for just $19.95.